D1245309

"All About Agile"

Agile Management Made Easy!

By Kelly Waters

Contents

INTRODUCTION   1

AGILE ADOPTION   3

AGILE MANIFESTO   5
DEFINITION OF AGILE - IN A NUTSHELL   7
AGILE DEVELOPMENT CYCLE   8
AGILE METHODOLOGIES   10
EXTREME PROGRAMMING IS NOT AGILE!   11
DISADVANTAGES OF AGILE   12
THE BEAUTY OF NOT DOING AGILE DEVELOPMENT   15
10 GOOD REASONS TO DO AGILE DEVELOPMENT   17
A SAD INDICTMENT OF THE SOFTWARE DEVELOPMENT INDUSTRY   20
AGILE SOFTWARE DEVELOPMENT SAVES LIVES!   22
AGILE DEVELOPMENT REACHES EVERY CORNER OF THE GLOBE   24
AGILE TRANSFORMATION   27

10 KEY PRINCIPLES OF AGILE   29

10 KEY PRINCIPLES OF AGILE   31
PRINCIPLE 1: ACTIVE USER INVOLVEMENT IS IMPERATIVE   34
PRINCIPLE 2: AGILE TEAMS MUST BE EMPOWERED   36
PRINCIPLE 3: TIME WAITS FOR NO MAN   38
PRINCIPLE 4: AGILE REQUIREMENTS ARE BARELY SUFFICIENT   41
PRINCIPLE 5: HOW DO YOU EAT AN ELEPHANT   44
PRINCIPLE 6: FAST BUT NOT SO FURIOUS   46
PRINCIPLE 7: DONE MEANS DONE!   49
PRINCIPLE 8: ENOUGH IS ENOUGH!   51
PRINCIPLE 9: AGILE TESTING IS NOT FOR DUMMIES   53
PRINCIPLE 10: NO PLACE FOR SNIPERS   55
BONUS PRINCIPLE 11: AGILE TEAMS LIVE AND LEARN   56

HOW TO IMPLEMENT SCRUM IN 10 EASY STEPS   59

EXTREME PROGRAMMING VERSUS SCRUM   61
WHAT IS SCRUM?   63
HOW TO IMPLEMENT SCRUM IN 10 EASY STEPS   65
STEP 1: GET YOUR BACKLOG IN ORDER   66

STEP 2: HOW TO ESTIMATE YOUR PRODUCT BACKLOG   71
STEP 3: SPRINT PLANNING (REQUIREMENTS)   76
STEP 4: SPRINT PLANNING (TASKS)   80
STEP 5: CREATE A COLLABORATIVE WORKSPACE   84
STEP 6: SPRINT!   89
STEP 7: STAND UP AND BE COUNTED!   93
STEP 8: TRACK PROGRESS WITH A DAILY BURNDOWN CHART   96
STEP 9: FINISH WHEN YOU SAID YOU WOULD   101
STEP 10: REVIEW, REFLECT, REPEAT   103

MORE ABOUT SCRUM   **107**

UNCOMMON SENSE   109
SCRUM HELL!   111
AGILE SCRUM, OR NOT-SO-AGILE SCRUM?   114
CERTIFIED SCRUM MASTER ISN'T WORTH THE PAPER IT'S WRITTEN ON   120
SCRUM: BAD LANGUAGE?   122
SCRUM AGILE DEVELOPMENT: IT'S A ZOO!   124
USING SCRUM ON LARGER PROJECTS: SCRUM OF SCRUMS   125

USER STORIES   **127**

SOFTWARE REQUIREMENTS ARE A COMMUNICATION PROBLEM   129
INTRODUCING USER STORIES   132
USER STORIES - ANSWERS ON A POSTCARD   134
EXAMPLE OF A USER STORY   135
'INVEST' IN GOOD USER STORIES   137
USER STORIES SHOULD BE *INDEPENDENT*   138
USER STORIES SHOULD BE *NEGOTIABLE*   139
USER STORIES SHOULD BE *VALUABLE*   141
USER STORIES SHOULD BE *ESTIMABLE*   143
USER STORIES SHOULD BE *SMALL*   145
USER STORIES SHOULD BE *TESTABLE*   147
USER STORIES VERSUS USE CASES   148
THAT'S NOT A USER STORY, THAT'S AN EPIC!   149
USER STORY THEMES   151
WRITING GOOD USER STORIES   153

AGILE ESTIMATING 155

AGILE ESTIMATING: THE SECRET TO DELIVERING ON TIME 157
WHAT IS THE POINT IN ESTIMATING? 159
ESTIMATING IN POINTS SEEMS A BIT STUPID! 160
AGILE ESTIMATING IN SCRUM - WHY ESTIMATE TWICE? 162
TO ESTIMATE OR NOT TO ESTIMATE? THAT IS THE QUESTION! 164
PLANNING POKER 166
AGILE ESTIMATING IN A NUTSHELL 168

AGILE TESTING 173

TEST DRIVEN DEVELOPMENT 175
DEVELOPERS CAN'T TEST FOR TOFFEE! 176
AGILE TESTING VERSUS WATERFALL TEST PHASES 179
THE CHANGING ROLE OF TESTERS 181
PUTTING THE *ANALYST* INTO TEST ANALYST 184

AGILE PROJECT MANAGEMENT 185

IS THE NEED FOR PROJECTS DEAD? 187
IS AGILE RIGHT FOR YOUR PROJECT? 189
AGILE PROJECT MANAGEMENT QUESTIONS ANSWERED 191
AGILE PROJECT MANAGEMENT IS NOT ENOUGH! 194
PMBOK AND AGILE 196
EXTENDING PMBOK 197
NO SPRINT IS AN ISLAND! 202
PRIORITISATION USING MoSCoW 204
HOW TO PRIORITISE QUICKLY AND INTUITIVELY 206
HOW TO PRIORITISE - GET MORE BANG FOR YOUR BUCK! 208
AGILE PROJECT INITIATION 209
AGILE PROJECT ELABORATION: SEED MONEY 211
THE PROBLEM WITH PLANNING 213
AGILE PROJECT PLANNING 215
TRACK SCOPE AND PROGRESS WITH A BURN-UP CHART 224
LARGE AGILE PROJECTS REQUIRE SOME NEW SKILLS 226
KEEPING SIGHT OF THE BIGGER PICTURE 227
HOW CAN I BE SURE MY AGILE PROJECT WILL DELIVER ON TIME? 230
MOST IT PROJECTS FAIL. WILL YOURS? 231
WHY MOST IT PROJECTS FAIL. HOW AGILE PRINCIPLES HELP 235

AGILE RISK MANAGEMENT   241
AGILE PORTFOLIO MANAGEMENT   243

LEAN   245

WHAT IS LEAN?   247
7 KEY PRINCIPLES OF LEAN SOFTWARE DEVELOPMENT   248
LEAN PRINCIPLE #1 - ELIMINATE WASTE   249
LEAN PRINCIPLE #2 - BUILD QUALITY IN   252
LEAN PRINCIPLE #3 - CREATE KNOWLEDGE   256
LEAN PRINCIPLE #4 - DEFER COMMITMENT   258
LEAN PRINCIPLE #5 - DELIVER FAST   260
LEAN PRINCIPLE #6 - RESPECT PEOPLE   263
LEAN PRINCIPLE #7 - OPTIMISE THE WHOLE   265
LESS IS THE NEW MORE!   267
KANBAN   269
MAXIMISING FLOW: WORK-IN-PROGRESS LIMITS   273
"TAKE THE TIME TO WRITE A SHORT LETTER"   277
DO LESS   278
IF YOU CHASE TWO RABBITS, YOU WON'T CATCH EITHER   280

AGILE TEAMS   281

ONE TEAM   283
AGILE TEAMS NEED TO PULL TOGETHER   285
CO-LOCATION   288
AGILE TEAMS NEED MANAGERS TOO!   290
20 SIMPLE THINGS YOU CAN DO TO BOOST YOUR AGILE CAREER   293
A FOOL WITH A TOOL IS STILL A FOOL!   294
AGILE TEAMS AT FULL STRETCH   295
OLD HABITS DIE HARD   296
AGILE GAMES - BALL POINT GAME   297
AGILE PRACTICES ARE MEANT TO BE ADAPTIVE   301
DEFINITION OF DONE! 10 POINT CHECKLIST   302
PAIR PROGRAMMING - AN EXTREMELY AGILE PRACTICE   303
TAKE RESPONSIBILITY   306
SELF-ORGANISATION IS NOT BOUNDARYLESS!   308
WHAT IF AN AGILE TEAM MEMBER WON'T PLAY BALL?   309
IT PEOPLE MIND YOUR LANGUAGE!   312
THE POWER OF A WHITEBOARD   313

AGILE LEADERSHIP   317

SELLING AGILE: GAINING COMMITMENT   319
WHY SHOULD YOUR BUSINESS CARE ABOUT AGILE?   321
SOFTWARE DELIVERY AS A COMPETITIVE ADVANTAGE   322
SOFTWARE COMPLEXITY + HUMAN FRAILTY + CHANGE = ???   324
CREATING A LEARNING ORGANISATION   325
7 REASONS CONTINUOUS DELIVERY NEEDS TO BE A BUSINESS INITIATIVE   327
20 QUALITIES OF AN AGILE LEADER   330
AGILE MANAGERS NEED TO TURN THEIR THINKING UPSIDE-DOWN   332
LOSE 25% OF DEVELOPERS WHEN MOVING TO AGILE?!   333
'THE POWER OF ONE' - CREATING AN AGILE ORGANISATION   334
THE VALUE OF PERSISTENT TEAMS   337
HOW TO SHARE AN AGILE TEAM   341
C3PO - A NEW ROLE MAYBE?   343
THINK BIG, START SMALL!   344
HOW AGILE ARE YOU?   345
MEASURING BUSINESS VALUE IN AGILE SOFTWARE DEVELOPMENT   349
METRICS   351
5 REASONS WHY AGILE DEVELOPMENT MUST BE DRIVEN FROM THE TOP   358
10 THINGS AGILE EXECUTIVES NEED TO DO DIFFERENTLY   362

FIND OUT MORE   367

ABOUT THE AUTHOR   369
FURTHER RECOMMENDED READING   371

Introduction

More than a decade since it began, 'what is agile' is still one of the most highly searched terms on the web.

Despite that fact, most books seem to concentrate on one particular aspect of agile methods, for example project management, testing, or something even more specialised like Scrum, Lean, Kanban, User Stories, Retrospectives, and many more.

As a result, I think agile methods often come across as much more complicated than they really are, and you have to read several books to get a good general understanding of all the key concepts.

By contrast, the purpose of this book is to provide a plain-talking comprehensive introduction to all aspects of agile in one place.

This book is a compilation of all the best educational content from my blog, allaboutagile.com. It's been organised by topic, so it's possible to read the whole book from cover to cover, but it's also possible to dip in and out as you please, reading pages of the book in bite-sized pieces.

Agile Adoption

Agile Manifesto

Many years ago, in a land far away, 3 wise men gathered to witness a birth. Not just any birth, but a birth that would be more significant than any other for many years to come. No, I'm not talking about the birth of Jesus Christ. I'm talking about the birth of Agile.

According to the agile manifesto, this is how it all started:

"On February 11-13, 2001, at The Lodge at Snowbird ski resort in the Wasatch mountains of Utah, seventeen people met to talk, ski, relax, and try to find common ground and of course, to eat. What emerged was the Agile Software Development Manifesto. Representatives from Extreme Programming, Scrum, DSDM, Adaptive Software Development, Crystal, Feature-Driven Development, Pragmatic Programming, and others sympathetic to the need for an alternative to documentation driven, heavyweight software development processes convened. A bigger gathering of organizational anarchists would be hard to find, so what emerged from this meeting was symbolic - a Manifesto for Agile Software Development signed by all participants."

The agile manifesto expresses some very simple philosophies. Simple, but very different to the traditional approaches to software development that went before. This is what it says:

"Manifesto for Agile Software Development
We are uncovering better ways of developing software. Through this work we have come to value:

Individuals and interactions over processes and tools
Working software over comprehensive documentation
Customer collaboration over contract negotiation
Responding to change over following a plan

That is, while there is value in the items on the right, we value the items on the left more."

Gradually, over the following decade, the manifesto gathered more and more support, and the use of agile methods grew increasingly popular. In more recent years, agile has been quite a phenomenon and one of the biggest buzzwords of the software industry.

While the individual methodologies existed before, this is when and how they came to be known collectively as 'Agile'.

Definition of Agile - In a Nutshell

Over the years, I have seen many bloggers attempt to describe agile methods succinctly, as it's not exactly easy to describe what it is at dinner parties! Not if you want to be left with any friends anyway!

The agile manifesto provides a fairly concise and good explanation for anyone really interested in the distinction between agile development and more traditional methods of software ⁄ development and project management.

But it's still a bit much for people with only a fleeting curiosity.

Where I personally struggle, is where a business person, a friend or associate asks casually, "what is agile?"

I know they're not really that interested. They certainly don't want to get into the whys and wherefores of software development practices. But they are curious and are asking more on a business-social level.

In these situations, it just asks for a one-line answer. One statement of what agile development is, what makes it different, why it is relevant. Boiled down to a simple statement. Agile development, in a nutshell.

I think the best I can do is this:

"Agile development is a different, more collaborative way of managing software projects, where the team delivers the product in small steps, allowing customers to make changes as needed".

Agile Development Cycle

Although agile development methods have been around for a little while now, many people still ask about the agile development cycle, what it is and how exactly it's different to a more traditional approach to development projects. Here is a simple explanation of the basics for people new to all this.

Traditional software development projects follow what is commonly known as a waterfall approach, where each phase of the software development life cycle is completed in detail and in sequence, one stage at a time. Simplistically a traditional software development life cycle might look something like this:

- Analysis
- Planning
- Design
- Development
- Testing
- Release
- Maintenance

With waterfall projects, the whole project is analysed, then designed, then developed, then tested, and then deployed. Sometimes projects are cut into multiple smaller phases to make them more manageable, but still these phases tend to work roughly sequentially like above and tend to still be quite large, for instance 3-6 months or often even more.

An agile development cycle is different. Instead, the initial analysis and planning is kept to a very high level, just enough to outline the scope of the project. Then the team goes through a series of iterations, analysing, designing, developing and testing each feature in turn within the iterations.

There aren't really any distinct stages during the development. Instead, each feature is taken from start to finish within an iteration, with the software ideally being released at the end of each iteration, or if appropriate even during an iteration.

An iteration is simply a fixed, short period of time that the team chooses to work within. Typically for agile teams, an iteration is between 1 and 4 weeks. Strictly speaking, the Scrum agile development methodology advocates 30 days, but I've encountered very few teams that actually do this. 2 or 3 weeks seems to be more common. The Extreme Programming agile methodology advocates 1 week. This is very short and in my experience requires quite a lot of maturity in the team and its processes to achieve, because getting to a stable release every week can be very difficult.

Either way, the principles are the same. The idea is to stick to short, fixed-length iterations and complete all stages of the development cycle for each feature in turn within an iteration.

The key difference this creates is visibility of complete working features much earlier in the project life cycle, allowing for a better gauge of progress and quality, and allowing for feedback and adaption along the way. The result is to see some results earlier, mitigate risk, and to allow flexibility to accommodate change.

One of the dangers of a waterfall approach is that by the time the detailed up-front planning, analysis and design are done, let alone by the time the solution is developed and tested, many requirements may have changed - especially these days when the pace of change is so incredibly fast. Agile mitigates this risk, helping to ensure that the right solution is delivered.

Agile Methodologies

There are various agile methodologies, although 'agile' is really more of a philosophy than a methodology. A set of values and principles. The agile manifesto describes these values and later I have summarised 10 key principles that underlie most agile methodologies. Agile methodologies are characterised as 'agile' when they exhibit these core principles.

Some examples of the most popular agile methodologies are as follows:

- **Scrum** - probably the most popular method globally and focuses on agile management and on how to better organise development teams.

- **XP (Extreme Programming)** - includes some management elements but emphasises technical practices more and is therefore more of an agile engineering methodology than Scrum.

- **DSDM** - Dynamic Systems Development Method, one of the earliest iterative development methods and more localised to the UK.

- **Lean/Kanban** - which focuses on cutting out as much waste as possible and retaining only the bare minimum process.

These seem to be the most widely adopted agile methodologies, however there are others, for instance:

- Crystal
- Feature Driven Development
- Enterprise Agile (previously XBreed)
- Agile Unified Process

Extreme Programming Is Not Agile!

In the course of my blogging, I've often come across comments or other bloggers talking about XP (Extreme Programming) as though it is agile.

Truth is, XP is Agile, but Agile is not XP...

Although I like a lot of the concepts in Extreme Programming, whether or not you use XP practices does not define whether or not you are doing agile development.

It's quite feasible that you're not doing Test Driven Development. That you're not doing Automated Unit Testing. That you're not doing Pair Programming. And that you're absolutely doing agile development.

Agile development is a set of values and principles. And Extreme Programming is just one of the agile methodologies that supports these principles.

People using Scrum are doing agile. People using DSDM are doing agile. People using 'home-made' forms of iterative, incremental, collaborative development are doing agile. To a greater or lesser extent, I admit, and with a different emphasis. But they are certainly 'doing agile'.

Extreme Programming, whilst one of the more popular forms of agile development, is only one form of agile development. And as it's name suggests, it is probably the most extreme. 'Milder' forms of agile can be equally beneficial, and should not be dismissed as 'not agile'.

Disadvantages of Agile

Don't get me wrong. I'm a big fan of agile development. If you're a regular reader of my blog, you'll know that.

But I'm not so pro-agile that I've lost all sense of balance. An agile approach to development is good for so many reasons. But agile development does require certain things that can also be a disadvantage.

If you're thinking of adopting agile principles, it's important that you know what you're in for. You need to be sure that you, your project team and the management supporting your project all understand these trade-offs, and are happy to accept and support them in preference to a more traditional approach.

Here's my list of potential disadvantages with agile:

1. Active user involvement and close collaboration are required throughout the development cycle. This is very engaging, rewarding and ensures delivery of the right product. It's the fundamental principle in agile that ensures expectations are well managed. And since the definition of failure is not meeting expectations, these are critical success factors for any project. However these principles are very demanding on the user representative's time and require a big commitment for the duration of the project.

2. Requirements emerge and evolve throughout the development. This creates the very meaning of agile - flexibility. Flexibility to change course as needed and to ensure delivery of the right product. There are two big flip sides to this principle though. One is the potential for scope creep, which we all know can create the risk of ever-lasting projects. The other is that there is much less predictability, at the start of the project and during, about what the project is actually going to deliver. This can make it harder to define a

business case for the project, and harder to negotiate fixed price projects. Without the maturity of a strong and clear vision, and the discipline of fixing timescales and trading scope, this is potentially very dangerous.

3. **Agile requirements are barely sufficient.** This eliminates wasted effort on deliverables that don't last (i.e. aren't part of the finished product), which saves time and therefore money. Requirements are clarified just in time for development and can be documented in much less detail due to the timeliness of conversations. However this can mean less information available to new starters in the team about features and how they should work. It can also create potential misunderstandings if the teamwork and communication aren't at their best, and difficulties for team members (especially testers) that are used to everything being defined up front. The belief in agile is that it's quicker to refactor the product along the way than to try to define everything completely up front, which is arguably impossible. And this risk is managed closely through the incremental approach to development and frequent delivery of product.

4. **Testing is integrated throughout the lifecycle.** This helps to ensure quality throughout the project without the need for a lengthy and unpredictable test phase at the end of the project. However it does imply that testers are needed throughout the project and this effectively increases the cost of resources on the project. This does have the effect of reducing some very significant risks, that have proven through research to cause many projects to fail. The cost of a long and unpredictable test phase can, in my experience of waterfall, cause huge unexpected costs when a project over-runs. However there is an additional cost to an agile project to adopt continuous testing form the start.

5. Frequent delivery of product and the need to sign off each feature as done before moving on to the next makes UAT (user acceptance testing) continuous and therefore potentially quite onerous. The users or product owner needs to be ready and available for prompt testing of the features as they are delivered and throughout the entire duration of the project. This can be quite time-consuming but helps drastically to ensure a quality product that meets user expectations.

6. Finally, common feedback is that agile development is rather intense for developers. The need to really complete each feature 100% within each iteration, and the relentlessness of iterations, can be a bit like being on a treadmill, so it's important to find a sustainable pace for the team.

I believe these trade-offs are well worthwhile. Software is complex. People are complex. And the only thing that's certain in projects is change. This lethal combination of unpredictability is more often than not helped by agile principles. So, in my view, for many project situations, the advantages of agile development far outweigh the disadvantages.

The Beauty of NOT Doing Agile

The beauty of NOT doing agile development... is that failure comes as a complete surprise, instead of being preceded by months of worry!

Often in traditional development projects, everything seems to be going so well, right up to 80% completion or perhaps even later.

Then things start getting harder.

Things start looking less and less likely to meet the planned end date. Until eventually you concede that you can't hit the date because it's just too late to do anything much about it.

In agile development, there are a few key principles that highlight issues early. Distressing though this is, the issues are highlighted whilst there's still time to do something about it.

One reason why this is a common problem in traditional software development projects is because the testing is one big lump all at the end. Consequently it's very hard to gauge quality until late in the day and it's very hard to judge how complete the product really is, because you don't know how many more bugs there are to find.

In agile development, testing is integrated throughout the lifecycle, features are completed one by one, and for each feature "done" really means DONE! In addition, the product owner or user representative is actively involved in order to see the product frequently and steer its development every step of the way.

All of these principles go a very long way to ensuring clear visibility of progress, and providing a clear and unambiguous measure of the product's completeness on a very regular basis.

That gives agile a big advantage over more traditional methods. An enormous advantage, actually. You get to see where the project really is, every day. And whenever you hit problems in a project, you actually see them, and see them when you might just have time to do something about it.

10 Good Reasons To Do Agile Development

I have personally experienced many advantages from successfully implementing agile methods. Here are 10 good reasons to apply agile development principles and practices:

1. Revenue
The iterative nature of agile development means features are delivered incrementally, enabling some benefits to be realised early as the product continues to develop.

2. Speed-to-market
Research suggests about 80% of all market leaders were first to market. As well as the higher revenue from incremental delivery, agile development philosophy also supports the notion of early and regular releases, and 'perpetual beta', enabling companies to potentially get their products to market earlier than competitors.

3. Quality
A key principle of agile development is that testing is integrated throughout the lifecycle, enabling regular inspection of the working product as it develops. This allows the product owner to make adjustments if necessary and gives the product team early sight of any quality issues.

4. Visibility
Agile development principles encourage active user involvement throughout the product's development and a very cooperative collaborative approach. This provides excellent visibility for key stakeholders, both of the project's progress and of the product itself, which in turn helps to ensure that expectations are effectively managed.

5. Risk Management
Small incremental releases made visible to the product owner and product team throughout its development help to identify any issues early and make it easier to respond to change. The clear

visibility in agile development helps to ensure that any necessary decisions can be taken at the earliest possible opportunity, while there's still time to make a difference to the outcome.

6. Flexibility / Agility

In traditional development projects, we write a big spec up-front and then tell business owners how expensive it is to change anything, particularly as the project goes on. In fear of scope creep and a never-ending project, we resist changes and put people through a change control committee to keep them to the essential minimum. Agile development principles are different. In agile development, change is accepted. In fact, it's expected. Because the one thing that's certain in life is change. Instead, the timescale is fixed and requirements emerge and evolve as the product is developed. Of course for this to work, it's imperative to have an actively involved stakeholder who understands this concept and makes the necessary trade-off decisions, trading existing scope for new.

7. Cost Control

The above approach of fixed timescales and evolving requirements enables a fixed budget. The scope of the product and its features are variable, rather than the cost.

8. Business Engagement/Customer Satisfaction

The active involvement of a user representative and/or product owner, the high visibility of the product and progress, and the flexibility to change when change is needed, create much better business engagement and customer satisfaction. This is an important benefit that can create much more positive and enduring working relationships.

9. Right Product

Above all other points, the ability for requirements to emerge and evolve, and the ability to embrace change (with the appropriate trade-offs), the team build the right product. It's all too common in more traditional projects to deliver a "successful" project in IT terms and find that the product is not what was expected, needed or hoped for. In agile development, the emphasis is absolutely on building the right product.

10. More Enjoyable!
The active involvement, cooperation and collaboration make agile development teams a much more enjoyable place for most people. Instead of big specs, we discuss requirements in workshops. Instead of lengthy status reports, we collaborate around a task-board discussing progress. Instead of long project plans and change management committees, we discuss what's right for the product and project and the team is empowered to make decisions. In my experience this makes it a much more rewarding approach for everyone. In turn this helps to create highly motivated, high performance teams that are highly cooperative.

Implications of embracing agile development principles
But there are implications. There's no such thing as a free lunch! And there's no magic bullet for software development. Sorry, no, you can't just drink the 'kool aid'! In exchange for all these benefits, you do get less predictability, software and humans are still difficult, you can't blame someone else if things don't go right. It generally requires much more commitment and effort from everyone involved - teamwork is even more important.

Nevertheless, the advantages of agile development are really compelling.

A Sad Indictment of the Software Development Industry

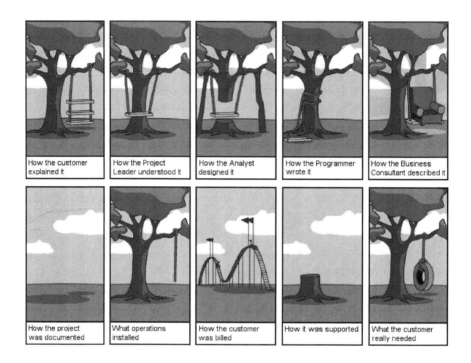

When I first saw this picture (many years ago now), it made me laugh. In fact I thought it was hilarious. A really humorous insight into one of the key issues in software development.

When I saw it again recently, to be honest it still made me laugh. But - when I thought about it a little more deeply - it also made me sad. Sad that the industry I take such a pride in being a part of, has this reputation. This reputation for delivering the wrong product! And that's just not funny.

The key principles of agile software development help enormously with so many of the common risks of project failure. Of course they don't alleviate all risks. Not at all. Because software development is complex. People are complex. And the combination of software and people is a lethal cocktail of unpredictability. But if there's one risk; one risk that agile software development really does guard against; it's this one.

The key principles of agile software development really do provide some insurance against this risk. The key principles of active user involvement, empowered teams, incremental development, frequent delivery of product, testing throughout, close collaboration, etc.

And if your product - like so many of mine, now and over the years - is a product that generates revenue - a product that is sold - then this benefit of agile, and this alone, can make the difference between success and failure.

Agile Software Development Saves Lives!

Ahem. Actually that's a bit of an exaggeration. I have to be honest with you. Agile software development probably doesn't really save lives. There, you heard it from me first. I just felt like being melodramatic...

Someone once joked with me that "agile is great, but you wouldn't use it on an air traffic control system!"

Actually, I would. In fact, I wouldn't dare use anything else.

But agile is just a concept - a set of values and principles. What specific agile practices would be most appropriate in a life or death situation like this?

Those who read my blog will know I'm a big fan of Scrum. I have used Scrum on its own, without any other agile practices, and with a great deal of success. I would probably still use Scrum as the management approach to an air traffic control system, but I certainly wouldn't use it on its own.

For a project like this, where quality is absolutely critical and lives depend on it, I would put a strong emphasis on XP (Extreme Programming).

Personally I would describe Scrum as an agile management method, whereas XP is more about agile engineering and XP has some important practices to assure quality.

One is Pair Programming. If we're going to write code that people's lives depend on, there's no way I would want a single line of code written by any one person. I would want every line scrutinised, every assumption challenged, and every line sanity-checked with a second pair of eyes. With Pair Programming, this level of continuous peer review comes as standard.

Another QA aspect of XP is automated unit testing and Test Driven Development (TDD). On a project like this, I would want 100% test coverage. I would want to know that every scenario had repeatable tests, so we could be completely sure that nothing ever regressed after passing the initial tests without us knowing about it. Anything less would simply be inadequate.

There are many specific practices in Scrum and XP that would help to mitigate risk and assure quality on a project as critical as an air traffic control system. But these two practices in particular - Pair Programming and Test Driven Development - if followed religiously, I am sure would deliver higher quality code than any other approach to development and testing.

In commercial situations, this level of rigour isn't always appropriate or affordable. But when quality is paramount, these engineering practices make complete sense. For an air traffic control system, the overhead of doing them 100% of the time is completely justified by the lives they could save.

In a situation like this, I wouldn't have it any other way.

Agile Development Reaches Every Corner of the Globe

Agile Software Development is a worldwide phenomena. My blog is testament to that. There's no reason for me to think that interest in agile development would be limited to only a few local areas. However, I've been amazed at how many countries my visitors have come from.

147 countries, no less!

147 countries including places I never imagined would be interested in agile development.

Everywhere from United States to the Far East, South America to Australasia, Skandanavia to Africa, Middle East to Eastern Europe. In fact every continent except Antarctica!

And virtually every country I've ever heard of, as well as some I haven't!

There's no doubt, agile is a global phenomenon.

10 Things I Hate About Agile Development

Love it or hate it, there's no doubt that agile development it's here to stay. I've enjoyed a great deal of success thanks to agile software development and agile project management methods, but here are 10 things I hate about Agile!

1. Saying you're doing Agile just because you're doing daily stand-ups. You're not doing agile. There is so much more to agile practices than this! Yet I'm surprised how often I've heard that story. It really is remarkable.

2. Worrying about the difference between 'Agile' (big A) and 'agile' (small a). You mean you spell it with a big A, omg you're so not cool! The differentiation is between Agile methods and being 'agile', in the true sense of the word. Most people probably don't get the subtlety. When people split hairs about this it gets on my nerves and makes so-called agilists sound like a bunch of overly-religious nerds.

3. Thinking that agile is a silver bullet and will solve all your problems. That's so naiive, of course it won't! Humans and software are a complex mix with any methodology, let alone with an added dose of organisational complexity. Agile development will probably help with many things, but it still requires a great deal of skill and there is no magic button.

4. Claiming to be Agile when you're clearly not 'agile'. Yes, we're doing all the major agile practices, but we're not flexible and we don't seem to understand the underlying agile principles. Were agile in practice but don't demonstrate the values of openness, attention to quality, collaboration, team spirit, etc.

5. People who are anti-agile but with nothing constructive to say about why. I hate that. I've had a few turn up on my blog and enlighten us all with their intellectual comments, such as 'snake oil' or 'agile is a hoax'. Losers!

6. Blaming agile - "I tried it once and didn't like it". Projects are difficult. Some projects may even fail, even if you are using agile methods. As I said earlier, agile is not a silver bullet. It's important not to blame agile when things go wrong, just as it's important not to claim it's the saviour for all of your ills. Don't blame the process. It's a bit like bad workmen blaming their tools. It's not big and it's not clever!

7. Using agile as an excuse - "no we can't do that, cos it's not Agile". "No I'm sorry, we don't do it that way here'. Following the agile process without fail regardless of the circumstances - even if it's contrary to what the situation really requires for the business or for the customer. If the process is the most important thing, that's not agile!

8. People who think they're smart enough to adapt agile processes before they've really got enough experience to understand how and *why* it works. It's an easy trap to fall into, but one that should be resisted. Otherwise it's so easy to throw the baby out with the bathwater!

9. People who use agile as an excuse for having no process or producing no documentation. If documents are required or useful, there's no reason why an agile development team shouldn't produce them. Just not all up-front; do it as required to support each feature or iteration. JFDI (Just F'ing Do It) is not agile!

10. People who know more about agile development than me. They're so smug ;-)

Ah, that's better! I feel much better now I've got that off my chest. Thank you for listening!

P.S. Oh, one more thing! I hate people who rant about agile development on agile blogs. That's just silly.

Agile Transformation

Talking about agile transformation is such a huge topic that I've often found myself trying to get my head around how to possibly explain it and where to start. In terms of my own experience, having successfully transformed two large media companies in the UK, I have found there are 6 broad areas that need to be addressed in order to make a successful transformation to a truly "agile organisation". They are shown on the image below:

The first is the **Vision**. Any transformation will always work best when there is a real business imperative. "If we don't change, we're out of business". "In order to survive, we need to be more responsive to customer needs and deliver value earlier". "In an increasingly competitive marketplace, we need to be quicker to market or we can't compete". I'm sure you get the picture! It helps enormously if that imperative is clear to everyone, articulated clearly from the very top of the organisation, and broadly bought into by staff. Of course it's possible that Agile isn't the solution, but I'm talking about cases where there is an acknowledged desire to become agile in response to these kinds of challenges.

The next 4 points are things that must all be addressed for a successful transformation:

Structure - the organisational structure may need to be changed to set the teams up for success in an agile environment. Small teams, business aligned, multi disciplined, ideally co-located, product oriented, shared goals, persistent teams, etc. This might also include changes to the recharge or funding model of the IT organisation.

Principles - of course this is the stuff about 'being agile', not just 'doing agile'. There are the 4 principles of the agile manifesto, the 7 principles of lean, and the 10 key principles of agile I've written about on my blog that attempt to extract the key principles underlying all major agile methodologies.

Practices - this is obviously the stuff about 'doing agile'. There are the most popular methodologies of Scrum, XP and Lean/Kanban, and the set of practices most commonly used by agile teams.

Technology - and then there's the need to invest in technology to support a more flexible, adaptive (agile) environment. Things like deployment automation, automated tests, continuous integration, and potentially an investment in architecture to make the applications more adaptive in nature.

Underpinning all of this is a need for **Leadership**. The courageous executive. Leadership to make all this change happen. And also a completely different style of leadership than we see in most large organisations whose traditional culture is command and control. This is the stuff Jim Highsmith touches on in his excellent paper 'Adaptive Leadership'.

Agile practices may be simple, but no wonder agile transformation is hard, especially if you're trying to make the change on a large scale and while in flight. It's not like changing the wheels of an aircraft while it's in flight, it's more like re-engineering the whole thing!

10 Key Principles of Agile

10 Key Principles of Agile

Here are 10 key principles that explain how agile development fundamentally differs from a more traditional waterfall approach to software development:

1. Active user involvement is imperative
2. The team must be empowered to make decisions
3. Requirements evolve but the timescale is fixed
4. Capture requirements at a high level; lightweight & visual
5. Develop small, incremental releases and iterate
6. Focus on frequent delivery of products
7. Complete each feature before moving on to the next
8. Apply the 80/20 rule
9. Testing is integrated throughout the project lifecycle
10. A collaborative & cooperative approach between all stakeholders is essential

There are various methodologies and standards that address various aspects of software development, for instance PRINCE2 for Project Management, Use Cases/UML (Unified Modeling Language) for Analysis and Design, ISEB for Testing. Although these are typically applied to waterfall development projects, elements of these methods can also be applied in an agile development approach.

There are also methods that are specifically designed around agile development and have a strong emphasis on the above principles.

DSDM (Dynamic Systems Development Method) is probably the original agile methodology. DSDM was around before the term 'Agile' was even invented, but is absolutely based on the principles we've now come to know as 'agile'.

Scrum is also an agile development method, which concentrates particularly on how to manage tasks within a team-based development environment.

XP (Extreme Programming) is a more radical agile methodology, focusing on the software development process and addressing the analysis, development and test phases, with novel approaches aimed at making a substantial difference to the quality of the end product.

DSDM is arguably the most complete agile methodology, whereas personally I believe Scrum and XP are much easier to implement. Scrum and XP are complementary, because they tackle different aspects of software development and are both founded on the same agile principles. One way of understanding how Scrum and XP are positioned differently is to think of Scrum as an agile management method and XP as an agile engineering method. Scrum and XP also overlap in areas, and it is common practice for agile teams to use elements of both Scrum and XP together.

There is a lot of hype about the transformational effects of agile software development. Personally I have found agile profoundly powerful in helping teams to deliver on time and building strong business relationships.

In reality, though, there is no magic bullet. The real trick is to know lots of techniques from various waterfall and agile development methods, and to select a mixture of the best approaches that are most appropriate for any given situation.

To do this reliably with any degree of success really requires a lot of experience and skill.

In agile projects, project management takes a slightly different form, relying more on the project manager's skills in communication, facilitation and coordination, emphasising more on people skills and less on planning and control.

Agile development can be a very exciting and invigorating approach, although some projects suit agile more than others. The collaboration and visibility can provide a much richer and more rewarding experience for teams to develop great software products.

Personally I think agile development can be a lot more enjoyable than the waterfall approach, which requires lots more documentation and is less flexible by nature. And when people enjoy their work, it's amazing what they can achieve!

Principle 1: Active User Involvement Is Imperative

Active user involvement is the first principle of agile software development.

It's not always possible to have users directly involved in development projects, particularly if the project is to build a product where the real end users will be external customers or consumers. In this event, it's imperative to have a senior and experienced user representative closely and actively involved throughout the project on a daily basis. Not convinced? Here are 13 reasons why!

1. High level requirements are clearly communicated and understood from the outset

2. Requirements are prioritised appropriately based on the needs of the user and the market, before much effort has been spent detailing them

3. Requirements can be clarified on a daily basis with the entire project team, rather than resorting to lengthy documents that aren't read or are potentially misunderstood

4. Emerging requirements can be factored into the development schedule as appropriate, with the impact and trade-off decisions clearly understood by all

5. Continuous feedback ensures that the right product is delivered. The product is more likely to meet user expectations

6. The product will be more intuitive and easy to use as a result

7. The user/business is seen to be interested in the development on a daily basis, which is very motivating and rewarding for the team

8. The user/business sees the commitment of the team and any challenges they face

9. Developers are accountable, sharing progress openly with the users/business every day, which builds strong relationships and a spirit of trust, openness and partnership

10. There is complete transparency as there is nothing to hide

11. The user/business shares responsibility for issues arising in development; it's not a customer-supplier relationship but a joint team effort to solve them

12. Timely decisions can be made about features, priorities, issues, and to decide when the product is ready

13. When the going gets tough, the whole team - business and technical - work together!

Principle 2: Agile Teams Must Be Empowered

An agile project team must include all the necessary team members to make decisions, and make them on a timely basis.

Active user involvement is one of the key principles to enable this, so the users or user representative from the business must be closely involved on a daily basis.

The project team must be empowered to make decisions in order to ensure that it is their responsibility to deliver the product and that they have complete ownership. Any interference with the project team is disruptive and reduces their motivation to deliver.

The team must establish and clarify the requirements together, prioritise them together, agree to the tasks required to deliver them together, and estimate the effort involved together.

It may seem expedient to skip this level of team involvement at the beginning. It's tempting to get a subset of the team to do this (maybe just the product owner and analyst), because it's much more efficient. Somehow we've all been trained over the years that we must be 100% efficient (or more!) and having the whole team involved in these kick-off steps seems a very expensive way to do things.

However this is a key principle for me and one of the critical success factors of agile. Doing these things together ensures the complete buy-in and commitment from the entire project team from the outset; something that later pays dividends. When challenges arise throughout the project, the team feels a real sense of ownership. And then this early involvement doesn't seem quite so expensive!

A common theme in agile methods is the idea of self-organisation or self-organising teams.

The concept is that the team is given full responsibility for delivery and the management role on the team, known as Scrum Master in Scrum, is a facilitator role.

The Scrum Master is responsible for orchestrating and enforcing the process (i.e. Scrum), and removing any impediments that hinder the team's progress.

For some, this is management. For others, management means telling people what to do and how to do it.

In reality, I think all teams benefit from this kind of light management style. It's empowering for team members. And, in my experience, empowered teams are more motivated and deliver better results.

However, empowered teams can also go in the wrong direction. To avoid this, a manager must coach and guide, and on occasions still enforce a particular direction.

Although self-organising teams are extremely empowered and tend to deliver great results, self-organising teams are also likely to have a much narrower view than their managers, who have broad exposure to all sorts of operational and organisational issues.

They may, for example, take a route that is contrary to important company policies. They may unknowingly take a route that has legal implications. They may take a route that suits the team and their current project, but is completely contradictory to some wider or longer term organisational goals.

So, whilst I believe strongly in servant leadership – believing that managers need to turn their thinking upside-down and work for their teams instead of the other way around – self-organisation is not boundaryless!

Principle 3: Time Waits For No Man

In agile development, requirements evolve, but timescales are fixed.

This is in stark contrast to a traditional development project, where one of the earliest goals is to capture all known requirements and baseline the scope so that any other changes are subject to change control.

Traditionally, IT professionals and users have been educated that it's much more expensive to change or add requirements during development or after the software is built.

Some organisations quote some impressive statistics designed to frighten users into freezing the scope. The result: It becomes absolutely imperative to include everything they can think of – in fact everything they ever dreamed of! Often the scope is then bloated into a huge wish list and it's easy to lose sight of what's really important.

What's more, it's all important for the first release, because we all know that Phase 2's are invariably hard to get approved once 80% of the benefits have been realised from Phase 1.

Ironically, users may actually use only a tiny proportion of any software product, perhaps as low as 20% or less, yet many projects start life with a bloated scope as a result of this approach.

In part, this is because no-one is really sure at the outset which 20% of the product their users will actually use. Equally, even if the requirements are carefully analysed and prioritised, it is impossible to think of everything, things change, and things are understood differently by different people.

Agile development works on a completely different premise. It works on the premise that requirements emerge and evolve, and that however much analysis and design you do, this will always be the case because you cannot really know for sure what you want until you see and use the software.

In the time you would have spent analysing and reviewing requirements, and designing a complete solution, external conditions could also have changed substantially. This is particularly true in fast moving markets of course, such as the web.

So if you believe that point – that no-one can really know fully what the right solution is at the outset when the requirements are written – it's inherently difficult, perhaps even practically impossible, to build the right solution using a traditional approach to software development.

Traditional projects fight change, with change control processes designed to minimise and resist change wherever possible. By contrast, agile development projects accept change. In fact they expect it. Because the only thing that's certain in life is change.

There are different mechanisms in agile development to handle this difficult reality. In agile projects, requirements are allowed to evolve, but the timescale is fixed. So to include a new requirement, or to change a requirement, the user or product owner must remove a comparable amount of work from the project's scope in order to accommodate the change.
This ensures that the team can remain focused on the agreed timescale, and allows the product to evolve into the right solution. It does, however, also pre-suppose that there are enough non-mandatory features included in the original timeframe to allow these trade-off decisions to occur without fundamentally compromising the end product.

So what does the business expect from its development teams? Deliver the agreed business requirements, on time and within budget, and of course to an acceptable quality.

All software development professionals will be well aware that you cannot realistically fix all of these factors and expect to meet expectations. Something must be variable in order for the project to succeed. In agile development, it's nearly always the scope (or features of the product) that are variable, not the cost and timescale.

Although the scope of an agile project is usually variable, it is acknowledged that only a small proportion of any product is actually imperative to the users. There is usually a relatively small set of core features and not all features of a product are really essential. For this philosophy to work, it's important to start development (dependencies permitting) with the core, highest priority features, making sure they are delivered in the earliest iterations.

Unlike most traditional software development projects, the result is that the business has a fixed budget, based on the resources it can afford to invest in the project, and can make plans for a launch date that is certain, even though the features may vary.

Principle 4: Agile Requirements Are Barely Sufficient

Agile development teams capture requirements at a high level and on a piecemeal basis, just-in-time for each feature to be developed.

Agile requirements are ideally visual and should be barely sufficient, i.e. the absolute minimum required to enable development and testing to proceed with reasonable efficiency. The rationale for this is to minimise the time spent on anything that doesn't actually form part of the end product.

Agile development can be mistaken by some as meaning there is no process. You just make things up as you go along – in other words, JFDI! (Just F*** Do It!). That approach is not so much agile as fragile!

Although agile development is much more flexible than more traditional development methodologies, agile development does nevertheless have quite a bit of rigour and is based on the fairly structured approach of lean manufacturing as pioneered by Toyota.

I personally believe that agile development teams can build better products if they have a reasonably clear idea of the overall requirements before setting out on development, so that incorrect design decisions don't lead the team down dead ends, and also so a sensible investment case can be made to get the project funded.

However, any requirements captured at the outset should be captured at a very high level and in a visual format, perhaps for example as a storyboard of some key parts of the user interface. In the early stages, requirements should be understood enough to determine the outline scope of the product and produce high level budgetary estimates and no more.

Ideally, agile development teams capture these high level requirements as a simple list of features (Product Backlog in Scrum).

They capture them in workshops, working together in a highly collaborative way so that all team members understand the requirements as well as each other. It is not necessarily the remit of one person, like the Business Analyst in more traditional projects, to gather the requirements independently and write them all down. It's a joint activity of the team that allows everyone to contribute, challenge and understand what's needed. And just as importantly, why it's needed.

XP (Extreme Programming) breaks requirements down into small bite-sized pieces called User Stories. These are fundamentally similar to Use Cases in more traditional methodologies, but are lightweight and more simplistic in their nature. User Stories are a very simple but very powerful concept.

An agile development team (including a key user or product owner from the business) visualises requirements in white-boarding sessions and creates storyboards (sequences of screen shots, visuals, sketches or wireframes) to show roughly how the solution will look and how the user's interaction will flow in the solution. There is no lengthy requirements document or specification unless there is an area of complexity that really warrants it. Otherwise the storyboards are just annotated and only where necessary.

A common approach amongst agile development teams is to represent each feature or user story on a card to allow them to be moved around easily as the work is completed.

Requirements are broken down into very small pieces in order to achieve this; and actually the fact it's going on a card forces it to be broken down small. The advantage this has over lengthy documentation is that it's extremely visual and tangible and encourages collaboration. You can stand around the whiteboard discussing progress, issues and priorities.

The timeframe of an agile development is fixed, whereas the features are variable. Should it be necessary to change priority or add new requirements into the project, the user or business representative physically has to remove a comparable amount of work from scope before they can place the new card into the project.

This is a big contrast to a common situation with more traditional projects, where the business owner sends numerous new and changed requirements by email and/or verbally, somehow expecting the new and existing features to still be delivered in the original timeframes. Traditional project teams that don't control changes can end up with the dreaded scope creep, one of the most common reasons for software development projects to fail.

Agile teams, by contrast, accept change; in fact they expect it. But they manage change by fixing the timescales and trading-off features. Cards can of course be backed up by documentation as appropriate, but always the principle of agile development is to document the bare minimum amount of information that will allow a feature to be developed, and always broken down into very small units.

Using the Scrum agile management practice, requirements (or features or user stories) are broken down into tasks of no more than 16 hours (i.e. 2 working days) and preferably no more than 8 hours, so progress can be measured objectively on a daily basis.

One thing I think should certainly be adopted from PRINCE2, the very non-agile project management methodology, is the idea of making sure all items are deliverables rather than activities or tasks. You can see a deliverable and "kick the tyres", in order to judge its quality and completeness. A task you cannot.

Principle 5: How Do You Eat An Elephant

How do you eat an elephant? One bite at a time! Likewise, agile software development projects are delivered in small bite-sized pieces, delivering small, incremental releases and iterating.

In more traditional software development projects, the (simplified) project lifecycle is in big phases: Analyse, Develop, Test - first gathering all known requirements for the whole product, then developing all elements of the software, then testing that the entire product is fit for release.

In agile software development, the cycle is Analyse, Develop, Test; Analyse, Develop, Test; and so on... doing all steps for each individual feature until it's 100% complete, one feature at a time.

Advantages of this iterative approach to software development include:

o   Reduced risk: clear visibility of what's completed to date throughout a project

o   Increased value: delivering some benefits early; being able to release the product whenever it's deemed good enough, rather than having to wait for all intended features to be ready

o   More flexibility/agility: you can change direction or adapt the next iterations based on actually seeing and using the software

o   Better cost management: if, like all-too-many software development projects, you run over budget, some value can still be realised; you don't have to scrap the whole thing if you run short of funds.

For this approach to be practical, each individual feature must be fully developed and tested, to the extent that it's potentially shippable, before moving on to the next feature.

Another practicality is to make sure that features are developed in priority order, not necessarily in a logical order by function. Otherwise, you could run out of time having built some of the less important features - as scope can vary and timescales are fixed.

Building the features of the software "broad but shallow" is also advisable for the same reason. Only when you've completed all of your must-have features, move on to the should-haves, and only then move on to the nice-to-haves. Otherwise you can get into a situation where your earlier features are functionally rich, whereas later features of the software are increasingly less sophisticated as time beings to run out.

Try to keep your product backlog or feature list expressed in terms of small features - not technical tasks. Ideally each item on the list should always be something of value to the user, and always deliverables rather than activities, so you can "kick the tyres" and judge their completeness, quality and readiness for release.

These are important characteristics of iterative, feature-driven development - and they're essential if you plan to deliver in fixed timescales - one of the 10 key principles of agile software development.

Principle 6: Fast But Not So Furious

Agile software development is all about frequent delivery of products. In a truly agile world, gone are the days of the 12 month project. In an agile world, a 3-6 month project is strategic!

Nowhere is this more true than on the web. The web is a fast moving place. And with the luxury of centrally hosted solutions, there's every opportunity to break what would have traditionally been a project into a list of features, and deliver incrementally on a very regular basis - ideally even feature by feature.

On the web, it's increasingly accepted for products to be released early (when they're basic, not when they're faulty!). Particularly in the Web 2.0 world, it's a kind of perpetual beta. In this situation, why wouldn't you want to derive some benefits early? Why wouldn't you want to hear real user/customer feedback before you build everything? Why wouldn't you want to look at your web metrics and see what works and what doesn't before building everything?

And this is only really possible due to some of the other important principles of agile development. The iterative approach, requirements being lightweight and captured just-in-time, being feature-driven, testing integrated throughout the lifecycle, and so on.

So how frequent is frequent? Scrum says break things into 30 day Sprints. That's certainly frequent compared to most traditional software development projects.

Consider a major back-office system in a large corporation, with traditional projects of 6-12 months or more, and all the implications of a big rollout and potentially training to hundreds of users. 30 days is a bit too frequent I think. The overhead of releasing the software is just too large to be practical on such a regular basis.

But consider a web site, a web-based product - or even more dynamic, something like my blog. There's no rollout overhead - it's an automated central deployment to all users, and for the blog it's a single click. No-one's paying for the service. If something's wrong, no-one dies. And it can be rolled back as quickly as it's deployed.

There may be thousands of users, even millions of users of a web site every month. But none of them need to be trained. And you can evaluate the impact on the user experience, and the user's behaviour through metrics within 24 hours and on an ongoing basis. In that scenario, 30 days is a lifetime!

Competitors won't wait. Speed-to-market is a significant competitive edge. The value of first-mover advantage is potentially enormous. Whilst it's not always the case, research shows that those first to market 80% of the time win in their space and end up clear market leaders.

So how frequent is frequent enough?

Think carefully about your own situation. Think about the two extremes I've described above. Think about what's right for you; your organisation; your product; your market; your customers. Think about what's right for you, in your particular situation. There is no right or wrong answer. Only what works for you, and what doesn't.

What is fairly important is to make this a positive decision to decide what's appropriate for you. And then to stick, if you can, to a regular release cycle. A regular release cycle allows you to plan. It allows your infrastructure and ops teams to plan. It allows your business colleagues to plan. It allows your launch events, marketing campaigns, etc to be planned. And because agile development works to a fixed timescale, these plans are assured, even if the precise features may vary.

A regular release cycle also allows you to learn more effectively. Your estimating might be good, it might be bad. Hopefully it's at least consistent. If you estimate your features using points to indicate their relative size, and track your velocity (how much of your estimate you actually deliver in each Sprint), in time you'll begin to understand your normal delivery rate. And when you understand this, you'll be surprised how predictable you can be.

And let's face it; managing expectations is really all about predictability. If people know what to expect, they're generally happy. If they don't, they're not happy. Maybe even furious!

So, one of the most important things in agile development is to focus on the frequent delivery of products. Or perhaps even more importantly, to focus on the consistent delivery of products.

Principle 7: Done Means DONE!

In agile development, "done" should really mean "DONE!".
Features developed within an iteration (Sprint in Scrum), should be
100% complete – i.e. potentially shippable – by the end of the Sprint.

Too often in software development, "done" doesn't really mean
DONE! It doesn't mean tested. It doesn't necessarily mean styled.
And it certainly doesn't usually mean accepted by the product
owner. It just means developed.

In an ideal situation, each iteration or Sprint should lead to a release
of the product. Certainly that's the case on BAU (Business As Usual)
changes to existing products. On projects it's not necessarily feasible
to do a release after every Sprint, simply because it's not necessarily
meaningful to ship part of a product.

However, completing each feature 100% in turn enables a very
precise view of progress and how far complete the overall project
really is or isn't.

So, in agile development, make sure that each feature is fully
developed, tested, styled, and accepted by the product owner before
counting it as DONE! And if there's any doubt about what activities
should or shouldn't be completed within the Sprint for each feature,
DONE should mean potentially shippable.

The feature may rely on other features being completed before the
product could really be shipped. But the feature on its own merit
should be of a shippable quality. If you're ever unsure about
whether or not a feature is really 'done', ask one simple question: "Is
this feature ready to be shipped?".

It's also important to really complete each feature before moving on
to the next...

Of course multiple features can be developed in parallel in a team situation. But within the work of each developer, do not move on to

a new feature until the last one is shippable. This is important toensure the overall product is in a shippable state at the end of the Sprint, not in a state where multiple features are 90% complete or untested, as is more usual in traditional development projects.

In agile development, "done" really should mean "DONE!".

Principle 8: Enough Is Enough!

Pareto's law is more commonly known as the 80/20 rule. The theory is about the laws of distribution and how many things have a similar distribution curve. This means that typically 80% of your results may actually come from only 20% of your efforts!

Pareto's law can be seen in many situations - not literally 80/20 but certainly the principle that the majority of your results will often come from the minority of your efforts.

So the really smart people are the people who can see, up-front without the benefit of hindsight, which 20% to focus on.

In agile development, we should try to apply the 80/20 rule as much as possible, seeking to focus on the important 20% of effort that gets the majority of the results as early as possible.

If the quality of your application isn't life-threatening, if you have control over the scope, and if speed-to-market is of primary importance, why not seek to deliver the important 80% of your product in just 20% of the time? In fact, in that particular scenario, you could ask why you would ever bother doing anything else?

Now that doesn't mean your product should be fundamentally flawed, a bad user experience, or full of faults. It just means that developing some features, or the richness of some features, is going the extra mile and has a diminishing return that may or may not be worthwhile.

So does that statement conflict with the last principle: "done" means DONE? Not really. Because within each Sprint or iteration, what you do choose to develop does need to be 100% complete and of a shippable quality within the iteration. This principle is about being careful about what you choose to develop, not about developing lower quality.

As a slight aside, I was at Microsoft for an executive briefing on some of their latest products. According to their own research, the average user of Word uses only 8% of the functionality. 8%! And I wouldn't mind betting at least 80% of us use the same 8% too! [assertion]. If Microsoft had developed only the important 8% of Word, maybe they could still have captured the same market share? Maybe, maybe not; sadly we will never know.

It's also worth considering the impact on user experience. Google has shown us that users often prefer apps that do just what they want. That's just what they want. And no more. The rest is arguably clutter and actually interferes with the user experience for only a limited benefit to a limited set of users.

So in an agile world, when you're developing a brand new product, think very hard about what your app is really all about. Could you take it to market with all the important features, or with features that are less functionally rich, in a fraction of the time?

Apart from reduced cost, reduced risk and higher benefits by being quicker to market, you also get to build on the first release of the product based on real customer feedback.

So all of this is really common sense I suppose. But it's amazing how often development teams, with all the right intentions, over-engineer their solution. Either technically, functionally, or both.

The really tough question, though, is can you see up-front which 20% is the important 20%? - the 20% that will deliver 80% of the results. In very many cases, the answer sadly is no.

Principle 9: Agile Testing Is Not For Dummies

In agile development, testing is integrated throughout the lifecycle; testing continuously throughout development. Agile development does not have a separate test phase as such. Developers are much more heavily engaged in testing; writing automated repeatable unit tests to validate their code.

Apart from being geared towards better quality software, this is also important to support the principle of small, iterative, incremental releases.

With automated repeatable unit tests, a lot of testing can be done as part of the build, ensuring that all features are working correctly each time the build is produced. And builds should be regular, at least daily, so integration testing can be done as you go along too. The purpose of this approach is to keep the software in releasable condition throughout the development, so it can be shipped whenever it's appropriate.

The XP (Extreme Programming) agile methodology goes further still. XP recommends test driven development, writing tests before writing the software. But, in my opinion, testing shouldn't only be done by developers throughout the development. There is still a very important role for professional testers, as we all know developers aren't always great at testing, particular when it's their own work they are checking.

The role of a tester can change considerably in an agile environment, into a role more akin to quality assurance than purely testing. This is compounded further by the lightweight approach to requirements in agile development, and the emphasis on conversation and collaboration to clarify requirements verbally rather than the traditional approach of specifications and documentation. Therefore there are considerable advantages to having testers involved from the outset in agile development.

Although requirements can be clarified in some detail in agile development (as long as they are done just-in-time and not all up-front), it is quite possible for this to result in some ambiguity or some cases where not all team members have the same understanding of the requirements.

So what does this mean for an agile tester? A common concern from testers moving to an agile development approach - particularly from those moving from a much more formal environment - is that they don't know precisely what they are testing for. They don't have a detailed spec to test against, so how can they possibly test it?

Even in a more traditional development environment, I always argued that testers could test that software meets a spec, and yet the product could still be poor quality, maybe because the requirement was poorly specified or because it was clearly written but just not a very good idea in the first place! A good spec does not necessarily make a good product.

In agile development, there's a belief that sometimes - maybe even often - these things are only really evident when the software can be seen running. By delivering small incremental releases and by measuring progress only by working software, the acid test is seeing the software up and running and only then can you really judge for sure whether or not it's good quality.

Agile testing therefore calls for more judgement from a tester, the application of more expertise about what is good and what is not, the ability to be more flexible and having the confidence to work more from your own knowledge of what good looks like. It's certainly not just a case of following a test script, making sure the software does what it says in the spec.

For all of these reasons, agile testing is not for dummies! Agile testing requires skill, expertise, judgement, and a passion for quality.

Principle 10: No Place For Snipers

Agile development relies on close cooperation and collaboration between all team members and stakeholders.

Agile principles include keeping requirements and documentation lightweight, and acknowledging that change is a normal and acceptable reality in software development. This makes close collaboration particularly important to clarify requirements just-in-time and to keep all team members (including the product owner) on the same wavelength throughout development.

You certainly can't do away with a big spec up-front and not have close collaboration. You need one or the other, that's for sure. A collaborative approach can be so much more effective and is so much more rewarding for all involved.

In situations where there is, or has been, tension between the development team and business people, bringing everyone close in an agile development approach is akin to a boxer keeping close to his opponent, so he can't throw the big punch!

But unlike boxing, the project/product team is working towards a shared goal, creating better teamwork, fostering team spirit, and building stronger, more cooperative relationships.

There are many reasons to consider the adoption of agile development; I have personally observed many business benefits with an agile approach. If business engagement is an issue for you, this is one good reason to adopt agile that you shouldn't ignore.

Bonus Principle 11: Agile Teams Live And Learn

When I first wrote my 10 Key Principles of Agile, unfortunately I forgot one. And I've now learnt that it's possible one of the most important of all, so I've decided to add it! So this is it. Bonus Principle 11: Agile Teams Live And Learn.

One of the fundamental principles of agile development is the idea of constant learning and feedback. The ability to frequently inspect and adapt.

There are two specific ways that agile practices help with this aim:

1. Frequent feedback loops
The first is frequent feedback loops. Frequent delivery of product, active user involvement, delivery of each feature in turn, regular review at the end of each Sprint or iteration. These are all practices designed to reduce the time between creation and feedback and speed up the feedback loop. This is important because it gives you the chance to get feedback about the product features while they are still in development and before too much has been done. This constant feedback can help to ensure that expectations and reality are kept in sync, the product can be adjusted to ensure it's the right product, and progress can be judged based on actual completion of features.

2. Retrospective
The second aspect of this is the practice of holding regular retrospectives. This is where the team meets at the end of every Sprint in order to discuss what's going well, what isn't, and what could be improved in the next iteration. This constant discussion about how to improve things as a team creates an open framework for learning and can lead to substantial improvements in the team's productivity. In fact, this aspect of agile is so valuable that I've often said to teams, if you implement nothing else from agile methods, implement the retrospective.

So with the frequent feedback loops and regular retrospectives, agile includes specific mechanisms to continuously improve both the product and the process.

It's also important for agile teams to foster a culture where they are not afraid to experiment. Fear of failure is one of the biggest inhibitors of people's performance, so it's important to do everything possible to make agile a safe place to experiment. It's okay to try something that doesn't work, because at the end of the iteration there will be another opportunity to discuss it and, if it isn't working, you can just change it.

The whole idea is that we learn by doing. We can spend ages trying to work out the 'best' thing to do, but in reality we will never know until we try it. The spirit of agile is to try something, monitor it closely, and constantly adapt.

There is a mantra in agile called 'Fail Fast'. This is where this phrase comes from. If you're going to fail, do it quickly, so you can adjust and get on the right track as fast as possible.

Obviously agile is not an excuse for repeated failure of the same type. No methodology or set of principles would support that. But it is okay to fail by trying something new, as long as we understand whether or not it's working within a short timeframe, and we learn from everything we do.

So this is how agile principles support the philosophy of continuous improvement. Agile teams live and learn!

How To Implement Scrum
In 10 Easy Steps

Extreme Programming Versus Scrum

So you've had enough of failed projects. You like the sound of agile development as an alternative. You buy into the key principles and you're ready to take the plunge.

Which methodology should you go for?

I don't have any official stats on which agile methodologies are most widely used, but there certainly seems to be much more of a buzz about Extreme Programming and Scrum, at least on a global basis, and surveys suggest that Scrum is the most widely adopted by some distance.

So which is right for you, Extreme Programming (XP) or Scrum?

I've heard a lot of people ask this question. I've heard people talk about them as though they are mutually exclusive choices. But really they are not.

They share the same underlying values described in the agile manifesto, and the same underlying principles that characterise 'agile'. They overlap in areas, but fundamentally they address different aspects of development.

Scrum is an agile management methodology. Whereas XP is more of an agile engineering methodology. As such they are entirely complementary.

If your motivation for adopting agile is wanting more visibility, better business engagement, team collaboration, a clear process for prioritisation, etc - Scrum is for you.

If your motivation for adopting agile is software quality, and better engineering practices - XP is for you.

In both cases you will benefit from a more incremental, iterative approach to development.

In my experience, Scrum is the more likely starting point when the adoption of agile is driven by management. And XP is the more likely starting point when the adoption of agile is driven by developers.

In my opinion, you would ideally do a combination of both. Or at least elements of both. And you would start with the one that addresses the issues causing you to adopt agile in the first place.

Nevertheless, Scrum is a good starting point. I have found it so because it is relatively easy to overlay straight over the top of your existing engineering practices, and is not constrained by technology in any way, as it simply tackles the management side of agile, not the engineering side. As such, it is easier to implement, hence why I believe it is more widely used and a good place to start.

What is Scrum?

If anyone thinks Scrum is now known to everyone involved in software development or project management, think again. 'What is Scrum' is still one of the most searched terms on the web (in relation to agile development that is).

According to the Scrum Alliance, "*Scrum is an agile framework for completing complex projects. Scrum originally was formalised for software development projects, but works well for any complex, innovative scope of work. The possibilities are endless. The Scrum framework is deceptively simple.*"

For me, that still doesn't describe what Scrum is. "*An agile framework for completing complex projects*" - I think that could be anything! Here is my attempt to define it more clearly:

Scrum is a simple and repeatable way of managing work. It can be used for projects, or for ongoing activities. It was originally designed for software development work, although is not specific to software development so can be used to manage any work.

Scrum is based on the principles and values of the agile manifesto, which proposes a different style for managing software development work, encouraging an emphasis on people over processes, working software over documentation, collaboration over contract negotiation, and responding to change over following a plan.

The term agile has also become synonymous with an incremental and iterative approach to software development.

Over the years, I have seen various diagrams that try to depict Scrum. In my opinion, they are not great because they often look over complicated to me, or they leave too much to the imagination. In an effort to address this, I have had a go at creating a clearer summary diagram for myself…

63

Here is my Scrummary :)

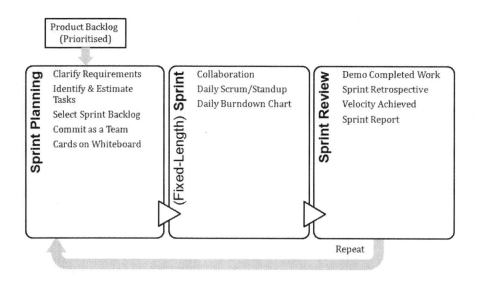

All of the activities referred to in the above diagram are covered in this chapter, How to Implement Scrum in 10 Easy Steps...

How To Implement Scrum In 10 Easy Steps

When I first encountered agile software development, I found it hard to understand. Okay, I might not be the brightest person you've ever met! But I'm not stupid either, I think!

There's a myriad of different approaches, principles, methods and terms, all of which are characterised as 'Agile'. And from my perspective, all this 'noise' makes agile development sound far harder, far more scientific, and far more confusing than it really is.

For this reason, I favour the Scrum methodology. Admittedly there's still a bit of jargon to learn. Otherwise, Scrum provides what is fundamentally a very simple way of managing software development more effectively.

Sure, it's great to have a deep understanding of the underlying values and principles of agile development. And it's great to have a thorough understanding of why Scrum works. And it's great to know lots of case studies where Scrum has been applied and try to relate them to your own individual situation.

But, fundamentally, I believe you can implement Scrum without all this knowledge. And still find many benefits and have a very positive experience of agile development.

In this chapter, I outline specifically how to implement Scrum in 10 easy steps.

Step 1: Get Your Backlog In Order

This is not only the first step to implementing Scrum, it's also the most important step.

Unless you can take this step, go no further. Do not skip it. If you do, I promise you'll regret it. Even if you get no further, this step is likely to benefit you, your team and your organisation.

First of all, where should you start?

Align with Business

Before you do anything else, you must align your development team with the business.

If you're part of a business unit, that might be natural and straightforward. If you're a central development organisation serving multiple business units, developing multiple products, it might be harder.

Initially, make sure you have at least one person dedicated to a product, application or product range where you will start implementing Scrum, where workload can be effectively prioritised by a single person.

You can certainly share a Scrum team across multiple products, but it's a little harder to manage and therefore is a slightly more advanced technique. If at all possible, it would be ideal to avoid this situation when you first start implementing Scrum, if you can.

Start with BAU

Secondly, although you can use Scrum on projects to good effect, I would suggest that you start with BAU (business-as-usual) rather than on big projects. This will keep things simple while you and your team get used to the basics.

So you've decided on a product where you will start using Scrum. You have at least one person who will be dedicated to that product (or product range). To keep things simple at first, you have selected a product that is in the BAU cycle of bug fixing and enhancements.

Find a Willing Product Owner

The next key step is to nominate a 'Product Owner'. You must find one Product Owner. One person who will be responsible for prioritising work on the product. One person who knows what is required of the product. One person that is a good communicator and able to convey requirements. One person who is committed to the success of the product, such that they are willing and able to dedicated a reasonable amount of time to its development.

That might seem like a lot to ask of any one person. But it's very important. If, for whatever reasons, this step is a problem for you, I suggest you tackle this issue before you continue.

If you can't complete this step, your product development is likely to be fraught with issues, whether or not you implement Scrum. Unless you can take the above steps, it's quite possible you will be faced with a barrage of requests, no clear view of priorities, a lack of clarity about requirements, lots of noise and complaints, and being pulled from pillar to post. The consequences? You don't deliver and/or fail to meet expectations. Everyone is miserable. And somehow it's all your fault!

Unfortunately, this situation is all too common for development teams everywhere. This must be solved before you proceed. This is a critical success factor for your team, with or without agile.

Act as Scrum Master

So now you're aligned. You have one product, application or product range. You have at least one person dedicated to the product ('Scrum Team'). You have one Product Owner. And you, by virtue of the fact that you're reading this information about implementing Scrum, I will assume are probably the Scrum Master, at least to start with.

As Scrum Master, you are responsible for supporting the Scrum Team, coaching and guiding them through this process, and removing any impediments blocking their progress.

Create the Product Backlog

Now you must create the 'Product Backlog'. Excel is an ideal tool for this.

As you're reading this, and I'm talking about nominating a Product Owner, you will probably need to create or facilitate the creation of the initial Product Backlog. Strictly speaking, it should be owned by the Product Owner. But you can get the ball rolling, and it's probably always best if the Product Backlog is really a collaborative effort.

The Product Backlog, in its simplest form, is a list of things that people want to be done to the product, in priority order.

Anyone can add anything to the Product Backlog. Anyone. The Scrum process, and agile development principles generally, are collaborative and inclusive. There is no longer any need to say no.

But, very importantly, only the Product Owner can prioritise the Product Backlog.

The Product Backlog can contain anything. Anything relating to the product that is. Bugs, enhancements, whole projects, issues, risks. Anything.

Having said that, items on the Product Backlog should ideally be expressed in business terms that are of some value to the user (or customer, or business). Not as technical tasks. Ideally every item on the Product Backlog should be a feature, not an activity.

Non-functional requirements, for example performance or security, can be put on the Product Backlog too. For instance, 'the product needs to be faster', 'we need to ensure the product is secure', 'we need to get off the old platform', 'there's a high risk of downtime due to a single point of failure'. These might not be features, as such, but they are completely justified as items on the Product Backlog.

Prioritise the Backlog

Next, with your help, the Product Owner prioritises the Product Backlog. They don't need to categorise the priorities 1, 2, 3 or anything like that. The priority is determined simply by the order of the list. The Product Owner simply puts the Product Backlog in priority order.

Things at the bottom of the list may be way off and may or may not ever get done. Things down the bottom are likely to be fuzzy and ill-defined. Don't waste time defining things you may never get to, or not get to for some time.

If something is a bad idea, the Product Owner should explain why they are removing it from the Product Backlog. However, if something's not such a bad idea, just never likely to be done, just put it in its rightfully low place on the Backlog and explain to the requester where it fits with priorities.

Actually this is just like queuing. Or standing in a line. We're all used to that. People will generally accept it. Providing the authority of the Product Owner has been communicated and has management support, people will generally take their place in the queue.

All too often in development teams, there is no clear visibility of the queue. People don't know how long the queue is. And they don't know how many are in front of them. This generally leads to impatience and complaints, because it's the only way to push in and get further up the line.

Visibility of the Product Backlog can make a substantial difference by solving, or at least alleviating, this problem.

The above steps can have a profound and powerful effect...

Prioritisation is now a business problem. The trade-off between adding cost and doing more, or waiting patiently in the queue, is now a commercial decision. A grown-up conversation about the cost versus benefit. It's no longer a delivery problem. It's a choice. Shouting loudest is no longer the system for prioritisation. So there is no point shouting.

And think about a technical issue or risk that causes you to lose sleep but you never get given the time to address. Put it on the Backlog. The Product Owner may decide that other, more visible features should take priority. But if the risk bites you, it was an informed business decision to carry the risk. Ownership of the risk is successfully transferred.

Things towards the top of the Product Backlog may be done in the foreseeable future. Therefore they are likely to be better understood. And they need to be well enough defined that the team could work on them. These features (or Backlog items) should be defined individually, so they can stand alone as discrete, deliverable pieces of work. Not part of a big network of inter-dependencies. And not part of a big specification document. Defined, yes. But defined in small, individual pieces. Clear definition of Backlog items just needs to stay one step ahead of the team. No further.

So there you have it. You now have a Scrum team. A Scrum Master. A Product Owner. And a Product Backlog. You've aligned your team with the business. You've created clear product ownership. You've got your team's work clearly prioritised. And you have a mechanism – a queuing system – for prioritising on an ongoing basis.

If you do no more, you will be better off for taking this step.

Step 2: How To Estimate Your Product Backlog

In step #1, I described how to get your backlog in order.

If you've completed step 1, congratulations! Because it's the biggest step, and the foundation for all else that follows.

If you haven't completed step 1 yet, I would advise you to go no further until you have.

Here's Step #2: How to estimate your Product Backlog...

High Level Estimates

You need to provide some high-level initial estimates, in order to get an idea of the size of your product backlog items.

This is helpful because it helps to inform the decision about priorities. And whether or not the features are likely to be worthwhile. From a management point of view, it also gives an indication about how big the team ought to be, commercials permitting.

But as yet, you don't know much about the items on the backlog. You don't know exactly what the features are meant to do. You don't know what tasks are needed to complete them. And you don't really know how you will implement them.

So you have to do a very high level, top-down, indicative estimate. In fact it's a guestimate, not an estimate at all really.

How many times have you heard someone say, 'don't worry, I won't hold you to it; I just need a rough idea'? And then they do hold you to it. Of course they do!

Estimate Product Backlog in Points

The answer: Estimate your product backlog in points. Not in units of time.

Repeat: Estimate your product backlog in points, not in units of time.

No, I haven't gone mad. I know it sounds a bit whacky. But I'm going to ask you to trust me on this one; it does have its reasons, some of which will only become clear later in the book.

In the meantime, I ask you to accept that development teams are more readily able to give guestimates of 'size', without giving an estimate in time that they might be held to, and without having all the gory details of every feature.

So we're not asking the team how long each feature will take. We're asking how big they are.

I also ask you to accept that Product Owners are more inclined to take this as a guestimate – as intended – and not as a premature commitment to a deadline.

Now of course I realise that points could be seen as useless to a Product Owner in terms of making a business case for funding. Certainly until a team has a track record and we know roughly how many points they tend to deliver in an iteration. But I'll come to that later. It is still helpful for prioritisation purposes and to get across the relative size of a feature to a Product Owner.

Use a Points System

So what scale should you use for your points system?

Personally I like Fibonacci numbers.

For clever people, take a look at the Fibonacci page on Wikipedia.

Mindboggling! For simpler people – like me – they're basically a sequence of numbers that some very old and very clever people (generally Italian, as per usual) have worked out have a slightly spooky, but very scientific significance. And this significance all relates to physics and the laws of distribution.

More about Fibonacci is really beyond the scope of this book, but they are a scientifically significant set of numbers, where each number is the sum of the previous two. They are:

1, 2, 3, 5, 8, 13, 21, 34, 55, etc...

It's significant that the number range becomes less precise as the numbers get bigger. That's why Fibonacci numbers suit estimating so much. As a piece of work gets bigger, your estimate is naturally less precise.

When using Fibonacci numbers to indicate the relative size of a feature, I would suggest you use the range 1 to 13. Certainly for bug fixes and enhancements on products in the BAU (Business As Usual) cycle, this should give you a sufficient range. Actually the smaller the range the better really. If you can break all your features down so small that you only need 1 to 8, all the better.

In any event, reserve 987 for that daft request you sometimes get to fly to the moon and back in an ice-cream carton!

The key here is about relativity. Here's an example...

A backlog item describes a feature. Maybe, for example, it's a report. You've done similar reports before, but it does have some complexity in the underlying data, so you decide to call this a 3.

Next on the backlog is another report. You size this one relative to the other one. Is it bigger or smaller? 2 is a bit smaller, 5 is a bit bigger. 13 is a lot bigger! And so on...

To make sure the scale works for you, I suggest you start by picking what you think is the smallest thing on the backlog. Give this a 1. Then find the thing you think is the biggest thing on the backlog. Give this a 13.

Now you have your markers, size the backlog items in turn, working from the top of the backlog using Fibonacci numbers.

When you get further down the backlog, you'll get to a point where the items are really rather fuzzy. And rather low priority in the scheme of things. In fact you may not be sure you'll ever get to them in your lifetime! Please don't feel you have to size the entire backlog. Size enough of the items to see you through the foreseeable future. Remember that the backlog has already been put in priority order, so make sure you work from the top.

Estimate as a Team

Size your backlog as a team. There's a whole philosophy about the wisdom of crowds. Two minds are better than one, etc, etc. If there are big differences between people's opinions, use this as a useful discussion point to understand why. Did one person see issues and complications the other person didn't? Did one person see a nice simple approach that others didn't?

You can also consider playing Planning Poker. This is a fun technique to ensure that people don't influence each other before giving their estimate.

Each team member writes their estimate (as a Fibonacci number) on a card, and everyone reveals their answer at the same time. This helps to ensure that less experienced members of the team are equally engaged and are not over-influenced by more experienced team members. It also helps less experienced estimators to learn from others. And it helps to avoid stronger, more vocal characters having too over-bearing an influence on the results. From this exercise, negotiate the size of each backlog item as a team.

Review Priorities

Once you've sized up the backlog - or enough of it - ask the Product Owner to have another quick look at priorities. Maybe now they can see the relative size of the features they've asked for, they might change their view of priorities. "Wow, if that's a 13, I'd rather have the other stuff first", or "if that's only a 2, let's get it in the next release". If any priorities are changed, simply move the item's position in the order of the backlog.

Stick with the Programme

Resist the urge to adapt this step. Ken Schwaber's book 'Agile Software Development with Scrum', which is highly recommended by the way, says this: "If you are not yet an expert in a subject matter (e.g. Scrum), do not attempt to adapt it. Scrum is an adaptive process. But you are in no position to adapt it until you know it well, and have experienced it in operation".

Sizing up your backlog using Fibonacci points is one thing I would encourage you not to adapt until you've tried it, and tried it over a period of several Sprints so you can start to see the powerful effects. Eventually, with the benefit of relativity, it's amazing how accurate you can be.

Step 3: Sprint Planning (Requirements)

If you've followed the first 2 steps in this chapter, you should now have your product backlog in order and have estimated the relative size of each feature using Fibonacci points.

The previous step is for estimating features at a high level when little is known about them. This is something you can do as items are added to the Product Backlog. Further details about specific features are only really gathered at the start of each Sprint, so no time is wasted on items that aren't being developed until later.

The next step - Step #3 - is to plan your Sprint...

Sprint Planning Workshop (Part 1)

Call a Sprint Planning meeting. Make sure the meeting is attended by the whole team. Include all roles. Business Analysts if you have them. Testers if you have them. All Developers on the Scrum team for the product. And very importantly, the Product Owner and any other important user representatives.

The first thing you must do (only in your first Sprint Planning meeting) is decide on your Sprint duration. This decision, like most others in agile, should be taken as a team.

Decide Your Sprint Duration

This is an important decision. Scrum suggests 30 days. It might be right. But this is one point that seems to be widely adapted by agile teams practicing Scrum.

The optimum Sprint duration depends on many factors. Something I read recently suggested that a development team's cycle time is a direct reflection of the maturity of their processes. I think I would agree with that statement.

A team with immature processes will find the intensity of Scrum and the overhead of Sprint Planning, Testing, Deployment and Review quite onerous for a short Sprint cycle. Whereas teams with very mature processes (for example automated testing, automated deployment, and teams who've become very quick at Sprint Planning), might be very comfortable with a short cycle.

I'd suggest the range is between 1 week and 1 month. 1 week is probably the shortest that will ever be practical, although if you really master agile practices, why not ship each new feature when it's ready? (if that's appropriate for the product). 1 month should certainly be the longest.

For fast-moving products or markets, such as web-based products – where there is a central deployment and no rollout or user training – 1 month seems like a lifetime! Personally I like 2 week Sprints for fast moving products.

Keep Sprint Duration Consistent

Whatever Sprint duration you choose to go for, my advice is to keep it consistent.

This, in fact, is more important than the length itself. Because it's this consistency that allows you to get into a rhythm. It's this consistency that makes your process very repeatable. And therefore helps you to get into your stride as a team. And it's this consistency that allows you to start understanding how many Product Backlog points you can typically do in a Sprint, making your delivery more predictable and therefore more reliable.

Once you've decided, you can set up your first Sprint Planning Workshop as a recurring appointment before every Sprint.

Select Target Sprint Backlog

Now you've decided on your Sprint duration. Next you need to decide on the goal(s) for the Sprint...

Looking at the top section of the Product Backlog, as it's in priority order, what would seem to be a reasonable goal to set for the Sprint? Can you express an objective that sums up the goal for the next Sprint, or at least pick a section of features from the top of the Product Backlog that the team thinks can be achieved in the Sprint duration?

Select your target backlog for the Sprint. Make this decision as a team.

Include a bit more than you think can be achieved. It's important to prepare more items during Sprint Planning in case the team finishes early. These items can be clearly identified as 'stretch tasks' and the Product Owner should not expect them to be completed. These are the things you will do only if the Sprint goes better than you expected.

In future Sprints, you will be able to use your Scrum team's previous Velocity to help with this decision. Velocity is the number of Product Backlog points delivered in a Sprint. This tends to fluctuate wildly early on when adopting Scrum. But it will settle down as the team gets into a rhythm, and within 3 or 4 Sprints should provide you with a reasonable norm to base your target backlog on.

Clarify Sprint Requirements

Take each item on the Product Backlog. It's important to go through them methodically, one item at a time.

The Product Owner presents each item and explains how he/she sees it working from a functional perspective.

The whole team discusses the item in detail. The whole team asks questions about the feature in order to establish what it should do and how it should work.

If someone has worked ahead of the Sprint and gathered some of this information, that is fine. Sprint Planning is about clarifying the requirements as a team. It's not necessarily the most productive approach to start from scratch in this meeting.

The outcomes of this discussion can be captured on a whiteboard or flipchart, or someone could write notes on a laptop as the discussion progresses. Interactive or printable whiteboards are ideal for this process.

You can use whatever form of writing requirements you want to. The important principle in Scrum, and in any agile development methodology, is that you write requirements feature by feature, just before they're developed.

Write requirements in a way that is lightweight and visual. Agile requirements should be barely sufficient and clarified at the time of development. The fact the features will be developed and tested within the next few days or weeks, and by the team that were present at the workshop, makes this possible.

Consider writing 'User Stories', a concept from XP (Extreme Programming). The basic concept of User Stories is to write features using this construct: "As a [type of user], I want to [do whatever], so I can [achieve what goal]".

The user story can be backed up by a quick sketch of the UI, a wireframe or visuals. Annotate the sketch to describe the functionality. Back it up with statements about how it will be confirmed (tested). This will help to identify scenarios up-front, before it's developed.

Next...

Once you have clarified the requirements for all the Product Backlog items targeted for your Sprint, the next step – Step #4 – is Sprint Planning Part 2 (Estimating Tasks). In this step you will plan the upcoming Sprint in detail...

Step 4: Sprint Planning (Tasks)

Once you've completed Step #3 and clarified the requirements for all of the Product Backlog items targeted for your Sprint, the next step is to plan the Sprint in detail...

Sprint Planning Workshop (Part 2)

The first part of the Sprint Planning Workshop (in the last step) was focused on clarifying requirements for the selected items on the Product Backlog. The second part of the Sprint Planning Workshop is focused on breaking those requirements into tasks and estimating the hours required to complete them.

Although Part 2 of the workshop can follow straight on from the first part, it is sometimes helpful for there to be a short gap between the two meetings; maybe 1 day. This allows time to clarify any outstanding questions arising from part 1 of the workshop before proceeding with the next step.

Make sure the meeting is attended by all team members. Include all roles. Business Analysts if you have them. Testers if you have them. All Developers on the Scrum team for the product.

The Product Owner and any customer, user or business representatives need not attend this part (part 2) of the Sprint Planning workshop, as it's likely to be more technical in nature and is more about the team working out how the selected backlog items will be delivered.

However, they should be welcome to attend if they wish, which may help their understanding of what's involved to deliver the features, and may help if any further clarification is required as the tasks are discussed and estimated.

Set the Sprint Budget

First of all, calculate the team's Sprint Budget. This is the available number of hours the team has to work on the Sprint.

Start by multiplying the available hours in the Sprint Duration by the number of full-time people in the Sprint. For people who are working part-time in the Sprint, include the number of hours they can commit to.

Then, make any reasonable deductions for time that team members will not be able to spend working on the Sprint. Deduct holidays, any known meetings, any time likely to be spent working on other projects, etc. Based on past experience, deduct a reasonable amount of time for support, if appropriate.

Make sure all these calculations are transparent and visible to all.

Break Requirements into Tasks

Go through each Product Backlog item selected for the Sprint and break them down into tasks.

Tasks may include the traditional steps in a development lifecycle (although limited to the feature in question, not the entire product). For instance, Design, Development, Unit Testing, System Testing, Acceptance Testing, Documentation, etc.

Remember, agile software development methods do not exclude these steps. Agile methods just advocate doing the steps feature-by-feature, just in time, instead of in big phases.

Each of these tasks, especially development, may be broken down further. Maybe to a component level detailing each of the individual elements of the software architecture that will be required to deliver the individual feature of the product.

Include all tasks necessary to make the Product Backlog item 100% complete – i.e. potentially shippable – within the Sprint. Agree as a team on your definition of done, so everyone is fully aware what will have to be completed and included in the estimates.

State tasks as deliverables, if at all possible. Deliverables are more measurable than tasks. Instead of describing what you're going to do, describe what you're going to deliver.

Estimate Tasks in Hours

Keep tasks small. Estimate all tasks in hours. Estimate each task as a team.

Ask everyone what they think, in order to identify missed tasks, or to identify simpler solutions.

Ideally task estimates should be no more than 1 day. If an estimate is much larger than this, the feature should be broken down further so the tasks are smaller. Although this can be difficult, it will get easier with practice.

Keeping tasks small enough to estimate at less than 1 day has some specific benefits...

Firstly, breaking tasks down into very small chunks means they are easier to estimate. The accuracy of your estimating will be improved as a result. Secondly, tasks less than 1 day are more measurable in the daily Scrum (stand-up meeting). By tomorrow, 1 day tasks are either done or they are not.

Commit to the Sprint Backlog

Add up all the task estimates for the Product Backlog items selected for the Sprint.

If they are significantly over the team's Sprint Budget, reduce the number of Product Backlog items selected for the Sprint. Remember the Product Backlog was in priority order, so if possible it should be the lower item(s) on the backlog that are removed from the Sprint.

The remaining list of estimated Tasks – those tasks needed to complete the selected Product Backlog within the Sprint - is known in Scrum as your 'Sprint Backlog'.

The team should decide together on how much to commit to delivering for the Sprint Backlog.

Identify Stretch Tasks

Sometimes teams under-commit or over-estimate.

In my experience, this is quite common when teams are new to Scrum. I think it's because they are unfamiliar with the process and potentially out of their comfort zone initially. They may not have had much experience of estimating in the past. And they may not have been asked to commit to their own delivery before. This can sometimes result in an over-cautious approach to the estimates.

Always include some additional scope in your Sprint Backlog, over and above what you think can be achieved. This is important in order to have something ready if the team delivers early, as the Sprint should ideally remain a fixed length.

Clearly identify these items as 'Stretch Tasks'. The Product Owner should never expect Stretch Tasks to be reached. No-one should ever be beaten up if Stretch Tasks are never reached. And if you do manage to complete any Stretch Tasks, this should be cause for celebration!

Next...

So now you've got your backlog in order, estimated your backlog, clarified your requirements, and planned your sprint. Now you're ready for Step #5 – Create a collaborative workspace...

Step 5: Create A Collaborative Workspace

I know I called this chapter '10 easy steps', but the first 4 are actually quite hard work! This one's a breeze, and just as important...

Whiteboard Your Walls

Cover your walls in whiteboards. You can't have too many!

A whiteboard beats tools for many purposes. High level plans, roadmaps, key dates, design discussions, sketches of functionality, issues, ideas, stats, status reports, topical posters, etc. You name it, stick it on the wall!

Create a Place for Collaboration

The whiteboard area will be your team's "collaboration hub". A visibility wall. The centre of all team discussions. The place where the team meets every day (standing up). The place where you can get everything you need to know, at a glance.

Management by Post-it Note

Mark up a whiteboard with 5 columns. You can add more if you want to. But at least do these. Label the columns: Sprint Backlog, Tasks To Do, Work In Progress, Ready To Be Verified and Done!

On a post-it note or card, write the reference number, name and description of each Product Backlog item that is included in the current Sprint. Put these in the left-most column, 'Sprint Backlog'. These notes don't need to fully describe the functionality or requirements. They're just reminders about what's included in the Sprint, and indications of progress.

Then write up a note for each Task on the Sprint Backlog. Place the Tasks beside their relevant Sprint Backlog items, in the column labelled 'Tasks To Do'.

When someone starts working on a Task, they should move it to the column labelled 'Work In Progress'. When it's ready to be verified, move it to the next column. When it's done, it should be moved to the 'Done!' column. Remember to define what your team means by done, maybe as a checklist.

This simplistic approach will create unrivalled visibility for you, the team, the product owner and any else that's interested.

Tactile

In my opinion, no software tool can replace the whiteboard. People have a special tactile relationship with the board.

Like email compared with face-to-face communication, no tool will replace the sense of collaboration and teamwork this focal point provides.

Yes, it might be more efficient to use a software tool. But efficiency isn't everything. Effectiveness is more important than efficiency.

For tactile people, it feels good to move a card to done. You feel a sense of ownership when you pick up a card. A business owner feels a greater sense of responsibility – real acknowledgement – when they add something to the board and take something else off the board to take it out of scope. It feels like something was actually, physically removed.

Visual

A whiteboard is also visual. And it's BIG. You can see at a glance how things are going.

When you're part way through a Sprint, and most of the cards are still on the left of the board, you know it's not going so well. Or you're coming towards the end of a Sprint, and the cards are mostly – reassuringly – on the right of the board, you know it's going fine.

The Burndown Chart (covered later) shows you instantly whether the team is on track. And, if not, by how much. All at a glance as you walk past the board. Whether you made a special effort to look or not. The visibility is unbeatable.

When you see something in print on the wall, somehow it seems more real. I guess because it's physical. A large number of post-it notes on a whiteboard looks like a lot of work. Probably because it is a lot of work! Its sheer physical presence reflects the amount of work the team is actually doing. It feels busy. It feels like a place where a lot is happening, which feels good. A long list of tasks on a project plan, or a long list of rows in a spreadsheet, simply doesn't have the same impact.

Because a whiteboard has no set structure, it suits the way many people think (though not all). Many people think visually. Not in lists, but in shapes, sizes, colours, etc. The whiteboard's lack of structure allows the information to be organised and presented however suits.

Important information can be highlighted easily by putting it on the whiteboard. Important information is not buried with loads of other documents and files in a project folder somewhere, which few people would browse and certainly wouldn't notice in passing.

Its visible nature can prompt people to remember things when they see them, rather than relying on their memory to go and look somewhere else that's out of sight.

Flexible

A whiteboard is also flexible. Infinitely flexible. You can put literally anything you like on it. Wherever you like. In any position, any size, any shape. Unlike an electronic system, there are never any constraints. No-one ever says you can't do something because the whiteboard won't let you.

It's fast and efficient to change. You could completely reorganise a set of cards in just a few moments. Or sketch something important in seconds.

Novel

It's also novel. When a team starts doing agile – and they create great visibility using the whiteboard – it's remarkable how many people want to come and look. Senior people have a sudden interest in what the team is doing. And even in the process itself. That would never happen with spreadsheets and tools! I can't ever remember a Director asking to come and walk through my project plan, or walk through my product backlog. In fact the very thought of it fills most people with dread! It just doesn't happen.

The whiteboard is interesting. It's interesting to look at. And it's interesting to talk about. When someone walks you through it, it's actually enjoyable.

Collaborative

Above all else, the whiteboard is a place for collaboration. It's a focal point. Like a campfire in days gone by. Or a fireplace in your lounge. Most team discussions happen round the whiteboard. Discussions about progress. Discussions about issues. Discussions about design. All sorts, sometimes even when the whiteboard isn't really needed. It becomes the hub of information for the team. The hub for communication and collaboration.

This is so much more than a progress board. It's an excuse for people to collaborate. And in development, where many people are not necessarily natural collaborators, it's an important step to get the team talking. To get the team working together. And to get them really working as a team.

Personal

And last but not least, the unstructured nature of the whiteboard allows it to be personalised by the team. The team can express itself through the things it puts on its whiteboard. It starts to show the character of the team, and therefore helps to create a visible sense of team spirit.

Tools

Tools can certainly help to organise information more efficiently. But I would challenge any tool to do all of that! I'm not against tools. Not at all. But I think they should supplement the whiteboard, not replace it.

Tools should be used for things they can do that a whiteboard can't. For instance, keeping track of longer lasting information, doing calculations, searching, providing visibility to people who can't physically be where the board is, etc.

But personally I don't think I'd ever use tools instead of a whiteboard. There's simply too much to lose.

Step 6: Sprint!

So you've got your backlog in order, estimated your backlog, clarified your requirements, planned your sprint and created a collaborative workspace. Now you're ready for Step #6 – Sprint!

Scrum does not really prescribe how you should go about delivering the tasks in your Sprint. Scrum is an agile management practice and doesn't really cover agile engineering. XP (Extreme Programming) on the other hand is an agile engineering practice.

In many ways, personally I think this is the beauty of Scrum.

Whatever engineering practices you use, from cowboy to rigorous, from RAD to RUP, from XP to DIY, whatever, Scrum can be laid straight over the top.

That's why I say it's easy. It's an alternative management approach. For projects and for BAU (Business As Usual). It's not a development approach, as such. That's why Scrum works even outside of development.

So, the team Sprints to achieve the Sprint Goal they committed to during the previous steps, moving the cards across the whiteboard as tasks progress.

Although Scrum does not prescribe anything much about how the team should do this, there are a few key principles of agile software development that I covered earlier that I want to highlight because they are particularly important to remember at this stage of the Scrum lifecycle...

Agile Teams Must Be Empowered

The Scrum team makes its own decisions during the Sprint. The team is empowered. Every time a manager steps in and makes a decision for the team, they remove some responsibility from the team. If a manager keeps doing this, the team gradually – piece by piece – loses ownership, along with their commitment. As a manager, the team must be given support, guidance, coaching and assistance. Not instructions. If necessary, the team should be helped to reach its own decisions.

Facilitation becomes a key skill for agile managers. Using their experience and management responsibility to help the team do its job. Not to do the team's job for them. Agile management requires servant leadership. Ideally inspirational leadership. The team self-organises to achieve its goals. But, remember, self-organisation is not boundaryless!

Time Waits For No Man

The timeframe – in this case the Sprint Duration – is fixed. You can add scope if you absolutely must, or add tasks if you discover they are needed. However changes in scope should be offset by compensating reductions in scope, i.e. removing something else from the Sprint. If you finish early, include more scope, i.e. the next most important thing on the Product Backlog. If you look like you're going to finish late, you must reduce scope in order to hit the deadline. But the end date does not change. At the end of the Sprint, the completed work is delivered.

"done" Means DONE!

In order to achieve a fixed timescale, it's imperative to make sure you complete one feature at a time before moving on to the next. You need to avoid reaching the end of the Sprint Duration with 90% of everything. 90% of everything allows you to deliver nothing. It's better to have 100% of something.

Testing is Integrated Throughout the Lifecycle

Achieving completeness – to make sure something is really done before moving on – means testing must be integrated throughout the lifecycle. In agile development, whether using Scrum or not, the traditional development lifecycle of analyse, design, develop, test, is repeated on a feature by feature basis, rather than in big phases for the entire project or product.

Testing starts at the start of the Sprint. In fact, it starts earlier than that. It starts in Sprint Planning, as involving testers at the start helps to clarify requirements. Writing the tests before a feature is built, means developers have more of a tendency to write the code to pass. Test driven development starts here.

No Interference Please

Ideally, once a Scrum team has committed to a Sprint, they should be left to focus on delivering what they've committed to. Constant changes to priorities prevent a development team from being fully productive and in the worst case can prevent a team from delivering at all.

If priorities must be changed during a Sprint, then so be it. However an equivalent piece of work must be removed from the Sprint to compensate.

Personally I like to educate Product Owners about the impact of chopping and changing by calculating changes at double the effort.

This is because the new piece of work was not discussed in Sprint Planning etc, and therefore all this has to be done in addition to the effort to implement the change. Doing this mid way through the Sprint is very disruptive. If you really must add 3 hours of development, maybe you should take 6 hours out to reflect this reality.

Aborting a Sprint

Aborting a Sprint is a very serious act and should be reserved for exceptionally rare circumstances.

Let's say the Sprint Goal is no longer applicable. Or something has come in that means we really need to re-focus the team completely. Or the Sprint or project is so far off track it really warrants a complete re-think.

These are the kinds of big events that should cause you to consider aborting a Sprint.

Aborting the Sprint means literally abandoning it and going back to Sprint Planning to re-assess priorities and re-plan.

Hopefully this situation is very rare, and ordinarily your Scrum team Sprints successfully to achieve the Sprint Goal.

Step 7: Stand Up And Be Counted!

So you've got your backlog in order, estimated your backlog, clarified your requirements, planned your sprint and created a collaborative workspace. You're sprinting to achieve your sprint goals. Now you're ready for Step #7 – Stand up and be counted!

Daily Scrum

Hold a daily stand-up meeting. The whole team must be present. It's not optional. The whole team must be involved. Including, very importantly, the Product Owner and any actively involved business, user or customer representatives. And any other people actively involved in the Sprint, even if they're not necessarily involved in the entire project.

Stand Up and Be Counted!

The team stands, in a half circle around their whiteboard. This is where Scrum gets its name. This is the Scrum.

Each team member reports back to the team in turn. Only the person reporting back should speak at one time.

Their report should be concise and focused. Their report should address 3 key questions:

1. What have they achieved since the last meeting? (yesterday)

2. What will they achieve before the next meeting? (tomorrow)

3. Is anything holding up their progress? ('impediments')

Quick questions can be answered there and then. But if any issues are raised as part of the report back, or if anyone has any questions that need further discussion, they should raise them but refrain from discussing them in detail until after the Scrum.

Only those needed for the discussion can stay back to discuss together after the Scrum meeting is finished. Everyone else can get back to work.

This is about very team member taking responsibility for their own work. Taking responsibility and reporting back to their peers.

Scrum Master Role

The Scrum Master is responsible for facilitating the Scrum meeting. Keeping it focused. Keeping it timely. Keeping it on topic.

The Scrum Master is also responsible for removing impediments. Impediments raised during the Scrum can be noted on the whiteboard for the Scrum Master to deal with.

The Scrum Master does not have to solve all impediments personally. They can delegate. But they are responsible for ensuring the impediments are addressed. And addressed quickly.

A key part of the Scrum Master's role is to protect the team and allow them to keep focused.

Same Time, Same Place

It doesn't particularly matter exactly when the meeting is. But it must be held in the same place, at the same time, every day. It must be routine. Like clockwork. So it must be at a time when all team members can usually attend.

Start On Time

Some agile teams agree a penalty for late arrival to the Scrum. Like most things in agile development, this should be a team decision. Often teams have a small fine for late arrival. This fine is paid to the Scrum Master and the team decides how to spend it at the end of a Sprint. Lateness usually stops as a result, and the team's time is not wasted!

Keep to 15 minutes

Stay focused on the purpose of the Scrum. With all team members present, it's an expensive meeting. You cannot afford for it to regularly overrun. It has to be brief and to the point. For practical reasons, and for everyone's sanity.

With practice, you should be able to keep it to 15 minutes, even with a large Scrum team, because the updates are little and often.

Step 8: Track Progress With A Daily Burndown Chart

So you've got your backlog in order, estimated your backlog, clarified your requirements, planned your sprint and created a collaborative workspace. You're sprinting to achieve your sprint goals and running daily stand-up meetings. Now you're ready to track progress with a daily burndown chart...

"Oh dear, it seemed to be going so well"

Often in traditional development projects, everything seems to be going so well, right up to 80% or 90% completion or perhaps even later. Then things start getting harder. Things start looking less and less likely to meet the planned end date. Until eventually you concede that you can't hit the date, and it's just too late to do anything much about it.

Agile Principles Help

In agile software development, there are a few key principles that highlight issues early. Distressing though this is, the issues are highlighted early whilst there's still time to do something about them!

One reason why this is a common problem in traditional software development projects is because the testing is one big lump all at the end. Consequently it's very hard to gauge quality until late in the day, and it's very hard to judge how complete the product really is, because you don't know how many more bugs there are to find.

In agile development, testing is integrated throughout the lifecycle, features are completed one by one, and for each feature "done" really means "DONE!". This means you have a very clear gauge of progress right the way through the project.

In addition, the Product Owner or user representative is actively involved in order to see the product frequently and steer its development every step of the way.

All of these principles, along with the daily stand-up meeting, go a very long way to ensuring clear visibility of progress, and providing a clear and unambiguous measure of the product's quality and completeness on a very regular basis.

Daily Burndown Chart

In addition to these principles, Scrum also offers a simple practice to track progress daily – the daily burndown chart – which beats any traditional project status report hands down in my view!

The daily burndown chart is a simple tool. But a very powerful one.

Estimated Time To Complete

In step 4, you created your Sprint Backlog – i.e. the list of backlog items targeted for the current Sprint, presumably in Excel. On your Sprint Backlog, enter the estimated time to complete, which of course at the beginning of the Sprint is the same as the original estimate.

Each team member can be responsible for updating their own ETC's on a daily basis before the Scrum. Updating it daily – and sharing the effort amongst the team – means typically there should only be 2 or 3 items to update for each person each day. Therefore it shouldn't be onerous and means team members take responsibility for their own tasks.

Be honest about what effort you believe is required to complete each task. That's the effort needed to get to "DONE!", regardless of how long has been spent to date and regardless of what was estimated in the first place.

Team Goal

The team's goal, quite simply, is for the team to reach zero hours to go, by the end of the Sprint duration.

Plot Progress Visually on a Graph

The beauty of this approach is that it's a numeric view of progress and can therefore be plotted visually on a graph. Plot the original estimates for the Sprint on one line, burning down to zero by the end of the Sprint. And the current estimates to complete on another line.

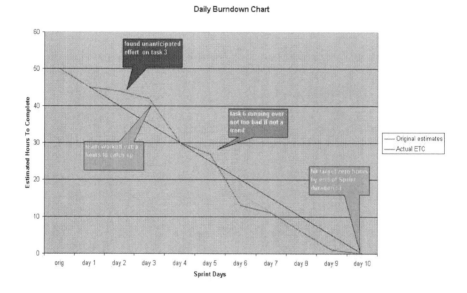

When the actual line tracks below the original estimate line, you're going faster than planned and on track. When the actual line tracks higher than the estimate line, you're running behind. It really is as simple as that! Highly visual, instant feedback for the whole team, every day.

Annotate with Key Events

I've also found it useful to annotate the graph with speech bubbles describing key events along the way. This is a useful way to record significant events so they're not forgotten by the time of the Sprint review (covered later).

It's also useful to highlight important things to management and stakeholders, instead of producing a separate status report.

Scrum Highlights Your Problems - It Doesn't Solve Them

Using a burndown chart, when you spend one day on a task and discover a whole load of problems or effort you hadn't anticipated or estimated for, the Estimate To Complete jumps up, creating an all-too-visual indicator of the problem for all to see.

When this happens early in a project, or on a large scale, believe me it's pretty scary! Suddenly you're not so sure about all this new-found visibility! It seemed like such a good idea at the time, but can you really stick that burndown chart on the wall?!

The burndown chart acts as an early warning system, making you aware of issues as soon as possible and allowing you the maximum possible time to do something about them.

Burn Down on DONE!

Some teams are naturally optimistic. In this case, they can have a tendency to fall behind, but compensate for this by being over-optimistic about the Estimates To Complete.

The consequence of this is that you still find you get stuck at the 80-90% mark towards the end of the Sprint, with no chance of sticking to your fixed timeline.

If you have this problem, consider burning down on 'DONE!', rather than on ETC. This simply means that you reduce the points to go on the daily burndown chart by the number of points in the 'DONE!' column. Until something is 100% complete, it doesn't score and it doesn't burn down.

This approach does tend to cause your burndown chart to go down in steps, where it stays flat for a while and only drops when all effort for a feature is completed. Whilst this gives you very clear visibility of what the status really is, it does also give you a slightly less granular view of where the team is up to.

You should choose whether you burn down on ETC or on DONE based on the characteristics of your team.

True Picture

Doing a daily burndown chart gives you a big advantage. You get to see where the project really is, every single day, in all its technicolour glory! When you hit problems in a project, you actually see it. And see it when you might just have time to do something about it.

Step 9: Finish When You Said You Would

So you've got your backlog in order, estimated your backlog, clarified your requirements, planned your sprint and created a collaborative workspace. You're sprinting to achieve your sprint goals, running daily stand-up meetings and you're tracking progress with a daily burndown chart.

Now you just need to finish when you said you would...

What a great idea! What an insight! If only I'd thought of that years ago, my development projects would never have been so hard!

Seriously though, there are a few key principles of agile software development that really help with this step. Here they are...

"done" Means DONE!

Okay, I've mentioned this principle quite a lot. It is really important. Complete each feature 100% before moving on to the next, so your software is always in a shippable state (subject to one last round of testing). Having all the features 80% complete is of no use to anyone. However, 80% of features 100% complete might well be a perfectly shippable product. Hang on to this principle.

Time Waits For No Man
Particularly on BAU (Business As Usual) product developments, you are usually in complete control of how many features, enhancements and bug fixes are in each release. If you hang on to the 'done' principle, you should be in a position to ship when your time is up, regardless of whether there are more or less items than planned.

All Changes Must Be Reversible

One of the key challenges in achieving this is to ensure your software is always in a shippable state, even when you have multiple streams of development (e.g. live bug fixes alongside major projects) on the go at the same time.

To achieve this, all changes must be reversible.

You must be able to routinely branch and merge your code, ensuring that you only take completed features at the end of the Sprint, and you're never caught with incomplete features on the main branch (trunk) of your code.

There's a phrase for this that might help your team to remember how important it is: "No Junk on the Trunk!".

Finish When You Said You Would

That's it. Complete each feature before moving on to the next. Stick to the principle "done" means DONE! Manage your code carefully so you can build a shippable product at any time. And even if it means varying the scope (that's varying scope, not varying quality), finish when you said you would.

Step 10: Review, Reflect, Repeat

So you've got your backlog in order, estimated your backlog, clarified your requirements, planned your sprint and created a collaborative workspace. You've sprinted to achieve your sprint goals, run daily stand-up meetings and tracked progress with a daily burndown chart. Now you've come to the end of your Sprint and finished when you said you would.

All that's left to do now is Review, Reflect and Repeat...

Sprint Review

At the end of the Sprint, hold a Sprint Review meeting. Invite the whole team. Invite all the key business stakeholders. Invite senior stakeholders including executives where appropriate. The more interested parties the better!

Review what was delivered in the Sprint. Demo the software. Whether it's complete, working software prior to a release, or work-in-progress in a longer-running multi-Sprint project, demo what has been completed in the Sprint. Let team members demo the areas they have worked on themselves.

The purpose of the Sprint Review is three-fold:

1. It allows team members to show what they've achieved and demonstrate their contribution to the product. They should hopefully be proud of what they've done.

2. It allows all key stakeholders to see what's been achieved, and provide valuable feedback on a regular basis, while there's still time to take it on board if it's part of a longer project.

3. It helps the team to stay focused on the deadline of the Sprint – noone wants to show up at the Sprint Review with nothing useful to show for themselves.

Sprint Retrospective

Following the Sprint Review, hold a Sprint Retrospective meeting. Invite the whole team. Invite the Product Owner. But this meeting is definitely not for the wider stakeholders. Typically it might follow on immediately from the Sprint Review, when the wider audience has gone.

The purpose of the Sprint Retrospective is to reflect on how things went during the Sprint. It's a chance for the team to discuss the Sprint and consider how they could improve things.

Together the team should:

*   Review the final Burndown Chart. How did it go? Did the team deliver what they committed to at the start of the Sprint? Reliability can be calculated as the percentage of planned points actually delivered. Note the team's reliability in a spreadsheet so the team's success rate can be plotted on a graph over time, to see if it's getting better or worse. This is a tool for the team to gauge its progress by. It's not a stick for management.

*   Review the team's Velocity. Velocity is the number of points delivered, based on the points given to the items on the original product backlog. Only items 100% complete, delivered and signed off count in the team's Velocity. There are no points for progress, only for completion. Again, plot this on a graph so the team's Velocity can be tracked over time, so the team can see if it's delivering more or less as time goes by. Velocity will gradually settle around a norm, and can then be used in Sprint Planning as a gauge for how much the team could realistically achieve, based on their track record. This helps the team to become very reliable at predicting what they can deliver in a Sprint.

- Discuss what went well (and try to make sure it's repeated next time).

- Discuss what could have gone better (and try to understand why).

- Decide what the team will do differently in the next Sprint. Try to pick a few actionable points that can actually be done differently immediately in the next Sprint.

This is a continuous learning process. Continuous improvement is built into Scrum.

Traditional project management methods also encourage continuous learning, through the production of a lessons learnt report on closure of the project.

The trouble with this is that people don't always remember enough by the end of a long project. Or perhaps there is so much to reflect on at the end of a large project, that there are too many things to consider and the result just isn't actionable. And often on completion of a traditional project, the project team disperses onto other projects or back to where they came from, preventing them from applying their learnings as a team.

In Scrum, continuous improvement is done frequently in small, bite-sized chunks. Little but often, just like the development itself. And while there is still time for the outcomes to have a positive impact on the rest of the project.

Repeat

The team is now armed with valuable information – about the product, about their performance, and about some of the impediments in their environment, for example:

- How the software looked after the last Sprint
- Feedback about the product developed so far
- To what extent the team was able to deliver what it committed to in Sprint Planning
- The team's Velocity and what is achievable in a typical iteration
- What went well
- What didn't go so well
- What will be done differently going forward

All that's left for the team to do now, is repeat the process, with the greater knowledge gained from above.

Realistically it takes 3 or 4 Sprints for the team to get into a rhythm; to apply the improvements and get used to the process. In this time, the team's Velocity will probably settle around a norm, and the team will really start to gel.

So that's it! That's basically Scrum, and how you can implement it in 10 easy steps.

Of course, the steps aren't really that easy in reality. The steps involve humans. And software. Which, as we all know, is a tricky combination!

Nevertheless, the Scrum process is inherently easy. And depending on your situation – certainly in my experience – Scrum and agile development can be a very enjoyable and rewarding experience, and help your success rate in many different ways.

More About Scrum

Uncommon Sense

Advanced Development Methodologies, Inc is the home of Scrum. On their web site, I recently noticed their strapline: 'It's about Common Sense'.

When you think about it, it really is. In fact, it's so ludicrously simple, it's almost funny.

Think about it.

Think about the basic framework of Scrum, only without the jargon:

- Make a list of the things you need to do (Product Backlog)
- Get someone (Product Owner) to decide what's most important and put the list in priority order
- Set a fixed deadline in the near future (Sprint)
- Estimate how much you'll be able to complete by the deadline (Sprint Planning/Sprint Backlog)
- Work through the list in priority order, completing each thing before moving on to the next
- Check your list every day to see how you're doing (Daily Scrum)
- Even if you haven't completed everything on the list, release the software when the time is up, in order to realise some benefits
- Review how it went to see if there's anything you would do differently in future (Retrospective)
- Repeat (iterate)

So if it's so simple - if it's such common sense - why do so many software development teams tend not to work this way?

Why instead do so many development teams tend to work on long projects? Seeking to understand and define the entire scope up-front. Seeking to resist change. Seeking to develop everything before testing it. Seeking to complete everything before releasing anything.

Perhaps the makers of Scrum should have tagged it 'Uncommon Sense'.

Personally I think that would be closer to the truth!

Scrum Hell!

When you first implement Scrum, it can be hell!

Sure, if you start with an established team, where the majority of the team has been trained in Scrum or done Scrum before, and you're working on BAU (Business As Usual), it's reasonably straightforward.

If you have a free choice about where to start implementing Scrum, I would highly recommend starting there.

But...

If you have a newly formed team, where the majority of the team has not done Scrum before or been on Scrum training, and you're working on a ground-up development project, implementing Scrum can be a painful and frustrating experience for everyone involved!

I have seen this situation quite a few times now. And without fail the experience seems to be the same.

Almost as much time is spent discussing the process and how things should be done as actually doing it. The Product Backlog is confusing and disorganised. Requirements are not clear. User Stories are not adequately prepared. Sprint Planning takes days instead of hours. And we all know how much developers love sitting in meetings!

Here are a few tips for handling this common situation...

First and foremost, get your backlog in order! In the earlier chapter about 'How to Implement Scrum in 10 easy steps', this is step #1 and the most important step. Here I say you should proceed no further until this step is completed, otherwise you'll regret it. It's true, believe me!

Accept the fact it will take your team at least 3 or 4 Sprints to get into any sort of rhythm. Refine how you handle the process in each Sprint.

Resist adapting the process. Ken Schwaber is the father of Scrum. Ken makes a very good point about this in his book 'Agile Software Development with SCRUM'. Scrum is designed to be adaptive. That's actually a key principle behind the method: 'Inspect and Adapt'. But until you understand a process well, and have some experiencing executing it as intended, you are in no position to adapt it.

Persevere. Trust me, it's worth it.

Apart from the usual issues when a group of people adopt a new process they aren't yet familiar with, newly-formed teams have their own challenges to overcome. According to research, a newly-formed team goes through some specific stages of team formation and only after some time does the team really begin to gel.

These stages are: forming, storming, norming, and performing.

During the forming stage, "supervisors need to be directive". This is in direct conflict with a key principle of Scrum, which is 'self-organisation'; the idea that the team is empowered and makes its own decisions. Until the team has properly formed, and the process has been established, the team is not in a position to do this.

During the storming stage, team members become more assertive and confront their colleagues with their views. This stage can be contentious, unpleasant and even painful to members of the team who are averse to conflict. Going through this stage whilst still learning how to execute Scrum effectively is what I would refer to as 'Scrum Hell'. It's difficult. But it's not possible to skip this stage. Human nature demands it.

The norming stage is where team members start to adjust their behaviour as they learn to work together as a team.

Some teams, but not all, will reach the performing stage.

These high-performing teams are able to function as a unit as they find ways to get the job done smoothly and effectively, without inappropriate conflict or the need for external supervision. Team members have become interdependent. By this time they are motivated and knowledgeable. The team members are now competent, autonomous and able to handle the decision-making process without supervision. Dissent is expected and allowed as long as it is constructive and channelled through means acceptable to the team.

Then, and possibly only then, is the team is truly capable of self-organisation.

Agile Scrum, Or Not-So-Agile Scrum?

Scrum is the form of agile software development that has helped me the most. It has helped me to transform the performance of the web development groups at two large media companies in London.

But, sometimes, I do wonder if Scrum is really agile enough?

There are quite a few regular meetings in Scrum. For short Sprints, this can be quite a big overhead. For me, that's where I can see why the Lean methodology appeals, especially to developers.

But there is also value in these meetings. So I thought I'd take a look at each Scrum meeting in turn, and assess whether or not their value really outweighs the effort?

First, there is Sprint Planning.

Sprint Planning happens before every Sprint. Often, that's generally every two or three weeks. In Scrum, this meeting is split into two parts...

The first part is to discuss the requirements for all the User Stories intended for the Sprint as a team and give everyone on the team the chance to understand what is required. Questions are asked, and hopefully answered, that give people useful insight into how each User Story will need to work.

Ambiguity is reduced and the team, hopefully, gains a common understanding of the User Stories and the requirements for the next Sprint. The collective experience of the team means that everyone gets the chance to input and the quality and appropriateness of the solution is potentially improved as a result. For a 2 week Sprint, this part of Sprint Planning generally takes about 2 hours, maybe less if the requirements for the relevant User Stories are well understood or well prepared beforehand.

114

Without this meeting, this discussion can still happen ad-hoc as and when someone picks up a User Story to develop. However, the chances are that the discussion will then occur with just the Product Owner, or perhaps one or two user representatives. It will be less onerous than having the whole team involved, that's for sure, but it won't benefit from the wisdom of crowds that you get from the group approach to Sprint Planning.

The other thing about this ad-hoc approach is that it's more onerous for the Product Owner. They would need to be available most of every day and at the beck and call of the development team. If your Product Owner is not full-time and sitting with the development team, Sprint Planning is a useful way to ensure sufficient access to their time, and it's a useful way to pre-plan this regular event in everyone's diaries.

Weighing all of this up, I personally believe Sprint Planning is costly (in terms of time) but really worthwhile.

The second part of Sprint Planning can happen immediately after the first part, although some teams leave a day or so's gap between the two meetings, in order to clarify any outstanding questions before going to the next stage. The purpose of this second part of Sprint Planning is to plan the Sprint in detail.

The idea is that the team works together to break down all the User Stories into tasks, and estimate each task in hours. The team then plans their capacity for the next Sprint and decides collectively how much to commit to in the Sprint.

Personally I think it is useful to think about the tasks for larger User Stories, but unnecessary to do this for the smaller or simpler ones. Although Scrum suggests estimating all of the tasks in hours and going through this detailed planning process, personally I think this has some negative effects...

Obviously it can potentially take quite a long time, and with the whole team involved, that makes it an expensive meeting. But I also think - ironically - it can really hinder a team's ability to deliver on time. There are two reasons for this.

Firstly, the team only estimates the tasks it can identify. They don't estimate the tasks they haven't identified. Inevitably there are some. Secondly, we all know by now that most developers are hopeless at estimating. Inevitably it their estimates will be wrong.

If you're on a large project, you may have already estimated all the User Stories on the Product Backlog in Points, in order to get an idea of how big the overall project is. If so, I personally think it's much more accurate for the team to commit to how many points they think they can deliver in the Sprint, and stick with that instead of estimating tasks in hours and trying to plan them in detail. In my experience, once a team's Velocity (the number of points delivered in a Sprint) has stabilised, this is a much more accurate way to gauge what a team can deliver in a Sprint, and it takes a lot less time to do.

If the User Stories being discussed in the first part of Sprint Planning have not yet been estimated in points, I would suggest the team voting on the size of each User Story once its requirements have been discussed. Planning Poker is a great technique for doing this.

So, in summary, my personal view of Sprint Planning is this: It is worthwhile to discuss the requirements for the intended User Stories for the next Sprint as a team. It is worthwhile to estimate the User Stories in points, either when they go onto the backlog, or using Planning Poker to estimate them as a team in Sprint Planning. It is worthwhile for the team to make a collective decision about the amount of points they are able to commit to for the next Sprint, based on their experience of their past Velocity. Whereas breaking every single story into tasks, aiming to identify every task, estimating each task in hours, working out the precise capacity of the team for the next Sprint, and committing based on that, is not necessarily worthwhile. It takes a long time and can lead to less predictability about what can be delivered, meaning the team doesn't deliver on its commitments and people are disappointed.

During the Sprint, the only regular meeting in Scrum is the Daily Scrum itself. This is where the whole team meets every day to answer three basic questions:

- What did you do yesterday?
- What are you going to do today?
- Is there anything blocking your progress?

This meeting should take between 5 and 15 minutes. No longer.

There is no doubt in my mind that the Daily Scrum is extremely worthwhile.

It keeps the whole team joined up and provides the Product Owner with clear visibility of progress and any issues affecting the team. This is one of the key ways that Scrum helps to ensure that development teams can keep stakeholder's expectations in line with their emerging reality. This is critically important. The definition of a successful project, at least in my mind, is one that meets or exceeds expectations. Therefore I would never personally suggest that a team does not have their Daily Scrum. It's a way to manage expectations on a very granular level, ensuring expectations and reality don't diverge along the way.

At the end of the Sprint, there are two more meetings: the Sprint Review and Sprint Retrospective.

These are useful meetings, but because they're at the end of the Sprint, they coincide with the Sprint Planning meeting which is at the start of the next Sprint. Sometimes this can make it seem like meeting overload for about 1 day of the Sprint, which to be honest can be a bit wearing.

The purpose of the Sprint Review meeting is to invite all interested people to come and see what the team has achieved in the last Sprint. If this is kept brief and informal, I think it's really nice for the team to show what they've done. It's also really nice for people interested in the project that can't be involved all the time to see what's going on and have the chance to provide regular feedback. This is another important mechanism to manage expectations in small, bite-sized pieces, which I've already mentioned I think is critically important to the success of any project. It's also a useful motivator for the team to achieve good results in each Sprint, as there will be a Review meeting afterwards so it tends to keep the team more focused on delivery.

And last but not least, the Sprint Retrospective. The purpose of the Retrospective is to build continuous improvement into the regular Sprint cycles. Again, there are three key questions to be discussed by the team in the Sprint Retrospective after each and every Sprint:

- What went well?
- What didn't?
- What will the team do differently in the next Sprint?

Doing these Retrospectives so regularly throughout a project means that the learnings actually help to improve the team's Velocity throughout the project (and beyond). If it's kept simple, the things the team want to do differently in the next Sprint should be actionable and should actually make a difference to the efficiency and wellbeing of the team and the project. There's no question this is a meeting you can't afford to give up. There's just too much value in it.

However, because it coincides with so many other meetings at the start and end of each Sprint, it's important to keep it brief. For a 2 week Sprint, half an hour should be plenty of time to quickly brainstorm these three questions and action any changes in the next Sprint.

So, in summary - whilst on the face of it all these meetings don't seem very agile, I do believe the Scrum meetings do help the team to be agile throughout each Sprint. They help the team to gain a common understanding of what's required, improving the quality of the solution. They help the team to have a common understanding of progress and issues, improving the level of teamwork and visibility for the wider team. They help the team to see what's been achieved, improving the level of satisfaction and helping to manage expectations. And they help the team to learn from past issues and improve on them in the very near future.

My conclusion? Talking takes time. But it also adds a lot of value.

Certified Scrum Master Isn't Worth The Paper It's Written On

In my opinion, Scrum Master Certification isn't worth the paper it's written on.

Don't get me wrong, I'm a big fan of Scrum. Huge fan. It's really helped me to transform the web development departments I have headed up.

And I'm not getting at the training companies that deliver Certified Scrum Master training either. Nor the people that go on the training.

But I do have a problem with the marketing of this training as 'Certified Scrum Master'. Because, to me, this phrase is completely misleading.

Over the years, I have come to think of the word 'Certified' as implying some depth of experience or knowledge. Maybe the passing of an exam following a period of study. Maybe a vocational assessment of someone's ability in the workplace. Something that validates a person's capability in the subject meets a minimum standard.

But with Certified Scrum Master training, there is no assessment or exam. No prerequisites for attending the course. No previous project management experience required. No study required. Simply attend a 2 day Scrum Master course and you are a Certified Scrum Master.

Secondly, the word 'Master' compounds the problem further.

I understand the word 'Master' in Scrum Master means 'master of ceremonies'. That's completely logical and makes perfect sense. However the word 'master' also happens to mean someone of 'great and exemplary skill, a worker qualified to teach others and carry on the craft independently; an expert in their craft'.

So, would you not really expect a Certified Scrum Master, or a Certified Master in any craft, to be someone at the top of their trade? Not someone who received a certificate of attendance following 2 days training.

Calling it Certified Scrum Master is a master class in marketing. And unfortunately I think it undermines Scrum - a methodology that otherwise can offer huge advantages to development teams of all disciplines.

So is Certified Scrum Master status worth having? Of course.

Is it worth going on the training? Of course.

Is it worth quoting your Certified Scrum Master status to current and potential employers? Of course.

But as a company practicing Scrum, I'm interested in people with Scrum training and more importantly, experience. It's important for employers to recognise Certified Scrum Master status for what it is - that is to signal that someone has been on the course. No more.

Scrum: Bad Language?

In Scrum, the list of work to be done (including bugs, enhancements, new features, whatever) is called the 'Product Backlog'. An iteration in Scrum is called a 'Sprint' and the work to be done in the Sprint is called the 'Sprint Backlog'.

Makes sense to me.

But there are some who are uncomfortable with the name 'Backlog' because it seems too negative. It seems as though the team is behind before it even starts!

In reality, of course, it is.

Because in software development, there will always be more work than you can possibly ever deliver, because with software there is no limit to what you could potentially do.

Therefore I think the term 'Backlog' makes complete sense. It helps your team, and more importantly it helps your Product Owners, to acknowledge the fact that you have limited resources and unlimited possibilities.

And then there's the benefit of a common language. Some argue that the terms don't really matter. Personally, I beg to differ.

Have you ever tried communicating when you're on holiday and don't speak the language? It's awkward, uncomfortable and tends to be error prone!

You might well argue that it's not as extreme as this... that's true. Not if you change just one term. But change too much and you do run a risk. You run the risk of losing the very clear benefits of a common language.

Scrum (and agile development generally) is an approach that relies heavily on close collaboration, teamwork and verbal communication. Therefore, I would personally recommend that you don't change the language unless there is a really compelling reason to do so.

Scrum Agile Development: It's a Zoo!

Many people find analogies a useful way to characterise new concepts, either to explain them to others or just as a way to remember them. If you like analogies, this one's straight from the top drawer!

In Scrum, the roles of Product Owner and Scrum Master are akin to a Zookeeper...

The Product Owner feeds the developers (with the Product Backlog).

The Scrum Master cleans up all the shit! (removes impediments).

Scrum Master anyone?!

Using Scrum on Larger Projects:
Scrum of Scrums

It is sometimes said that agile software development methods, such as Scrum, are ideal for small projects being delivered by small teams.

Personally I would certainly agree that Scrum is ideal for small, multi-disciplined, co-located teams, working on a common purpose.

However, these days we hear plenty of examples of larger companies using Scrum on a fairly large scale. I seem to recall Yahoo in particular once stated they were using Scrum agile project management on a project with 700 developers!

Of course it is relatively straightforward to scale Scrum up when the teams are basically a collection of small unrelated teams, each using Scrum but working on different projects. But what about when you need a very large team working on a single project, or on closely related projects in a large programme?

One technique for handling this - although I'm sure it's not enough on it's own by the way - is a technique called 'Scrum of Scrums'.

The concept is simple. Each team meets every day and holds their daily Scrum as usual. One or two representatives from each Scrum team attend a higher level Scrum to coordinate across teams. And on very large teams, one or two representatives from the higher level Scrum attends an even higher level Scrum, and so on.

It means some people need to attend two Scrums, but the Scrum of Scrums technique scales up very well and is easy to see how important information can be quickly cascaded all the way up the line on very large projects.

But the information that needs to be communicated, and the frequency of communication, shifts as you go up the line, and the process for a Scrum of Scrums needs to be slightly different from a usual Scrum.

Instead of the usual kind of update given at a Daily Scrum meeting, a broader, higher level view of progress should be communicated. There should be more emphasis on blockers, in case other teams can help and to recognise blockers that affect all teams. And there should be more emphasis on dependencies, especially those areas where the teams are reliant on each other.

User Stories

Software Requirements Are A Communication Problem

Let's face it. There is no perfect solution. No perfect solution for humans to share information accurately, consistently between multiple people, and over a prolonged period of time.
Especially when you add into that equation the level of detail that's needed to capture the requirements for a major software application.

And then there's the complexity of software. And the fact it's plyable. Its evolutionary nature means it simply isn't comparable to the creation of many other products. And certainly not comparable to construction projects, where once built the requirements are literally fixed in stone.

Software requirements, therefore, are a uniquely challenging communication problem. Such a challenging problem, we mustn't kid ourselves into thinking there's a solution. Personally, I am pretty sure there is not. However, there are ways of mitigating some of the problems, whether it's in written or verbal form. Let's look at some of the pros and cons of each...

Written Requirements
- Can be well thought through, reviewed and edited
- Provide a permanent record
- Are more easily share with groups of people

But:
- Time consuming to produce
- May be less relevant or superseded over time
- Can be easily misinterpreted

Verbal Requirements
- Provide opportunity for instantaneous feedback and clarification
- Are an information-packed exchange
- Can be easier to clarify and gain common understanding

- Are more easily adapted to information known at the time
- Can spark ideas about problems and opportunities

But:

- Are spur-of-the-moment and not always well thought through
- Are harder to share across groups of people, particularly if not co-located
- Conversations can be remembered differently by different people, or easily forgotten

Whichever form of requirements capture you prefer, we must all remember the old addage: "A picture is worth a thousand words". It's so true. Whether it's a diagram in a spec, or a sketch on a whiteboard, pictures add a dimension that is immensely valuable.

A common approach in agile teams is to use User Stories (explained later). User Stories seeks to combine the strengths of written and verbal communication, supported by a picture where possible.

And some key principles of agile development seek to address some of the weaknesses of both forms of communication, in an effort to create a best of both worlds:

- Active user involvement to ensure continuous visibility and feedback

- Agile teams must be empowered to make decisions, so details can be clarified at the time of development

- An acceptance that requirements emerge and evolve as the software is developed

- Agile requirements are 'barely sufficient', so they are not too onerous to produce and the latest information can be incorporated at the time of development

- Requirements are developed in small bite-sized pieces, so details can be captured verbally whilst minimising the risks of people forgetting details or not being involved when the requirements are developed

- Enough's enough - apply the 80/20 rule; capturing every detail isn't necessary to produce a quality product; verbal clarification, visible software and feedback works better

- Cooperation, collaboration and communication is essential between all team members, as everyone involved must know the outcome of any discussions about requirements.

Introducing User Stories

One of the most popular ways of capturing requirements in agile projects is to use User Stories.

User Stories are a simple way of capturing user requirements throughout a project - an alternative to writing lengthy requirements specifications all up-front.

User Stories are derived from XP (Extreme Programming), however they can just as easily be used for requirements gathering in any agile development methodology, or indeed in any home-grown development process. It is now common practice for agile teams to use User Stories within Scrum.

A User Story is a simple statement about what a user wants to do with a feature of the software, written from a user's perspective. A User Story should not use technical jargon or state design goals. User Stories should be written in business language that is understandable to all.

A User Story should focus on the who, what and why of a feature, not how.

For example, on a job site, two high-level User Stories might be:

1. As a job seeker, I want to search for a job, so I can advance my career.
2. As a recruiter, I want to post a job vacancy, so I can find a new team member.

This is a useful construct to give a consistent shape to User Stories, and to act as a constant reminder to focus on who, what and why:

As a [user role], I want to [goal], so I can [reason].

Some people may consider the third part of the construct to be unnecessary. However I think it's good to state the user's motivation for using the feature, because it:

- Gives clarity as to why a feature is useful
- Can influence how a feature should function
- Can give you ideas for other useful features that support the user's goals
- Can help to see simpler ways of achieving the same goal

At the start of a project, capture an initial list of User Stories up-front. In Scrum this would be the initial Product Backlog. This feature list is useful for estimating and planning. But defer capturing all the details until the story is prioritised and due to be developed in the next Sprint or iteration.

In meetings with users (or user representatives), users will often tell stories about the failings of their current system or process. Or they might tell stories about how they see things working better in future. Try capturing these stories as User Stories on cards while you're in the meeting, as they are told.

In traditional development projects, these stories often aren't captured as they are told, they're captured in a lengthy analysis process and captured in a lengthy document; a format that isn't particularly user friendly.

Using User Stories, you might be surprised just how easy it is to leave a meeting with users with their key requirements, or at least their goals, already captured.

User Stories - Answers On A Postcard

If you're capturing user requirements using User Stories, write them on a postcard (a blank one of course!).

A User Story Card should ideally comprise 3 parts: Card, Conversation and Confirmation...

Card
The heading section of the card should include the name of the user story, reference number and the estimated size in points.

Conversation
Most of the front of the card should include further information about the user story and what the software is meant to do. This can be a sketch or diagram of the feature, or notes about how it should function. Anything that helps to concisely explain the feature. Remember this is a reminder of the story and notes about it, not a full specification on a card. The team should collaborate to get more details at the time of development.

Confirmation
Write test cases or acceptance criteria on the back of the card. Writing tests up-front helps to ensure the software is designed to pass. Writing tests up-front also helps to identify scenarios that users, developers and/or analysts may not have thought of.

Keeping User Stories small enough to fit on a card helps to ensure that requirements are broken into small, manageable pieces of functionality, i.e. individual features.

Cards also work nicely in conjunction with whiteboards, providing clear visibility of progress and enabling team collaboration, moving cards around the board as things progress.

Example Of A User Story

Here is an example of a User Story card. It's quite a formal example as it has a wireframe on it, rather than just handwritten notes. I'm not really sure if you would consider this example to be good, bad or indifferent - I guess it depends what you're used to, but it is an example nevertheless!

This is the front of the card:

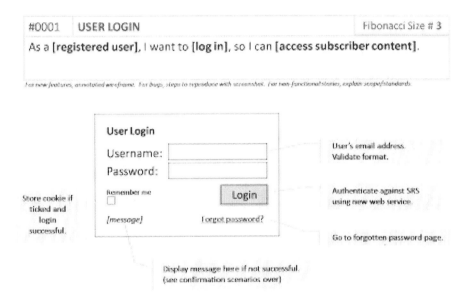

The Card section describes the user story. The Conversation section provides more information about the feature. Note the feature (for a user to log in to a web site) is small, so the story can be fairly well described on a small card. Clearly it's not as detailed as a traditional specification, but annotating a visual representation of a small feature at a time, makes it fairly self explanatory for team members. And I would certainly argue it's more easily digestible than a lengthy specification, especially for business colleagues.

Here is the back of the card:

Confirmation

1. Success – valid user logged in and referred to home page.
    a. 'Remember me' ticked – store cookie / automatic login next time.
    b. 'Remember me' not ticked – force login next time.

2. Failure – display message:
    a) "Email address in wrong format"
    b) "Unrecognised user name, please try again"
    c) "Incorrect password, please try again"
    d) "Service unavailable, please try again"
    e) Account has expired – refer to account renewal sales page.

The back of the card outlines the test cases for this feature - how it's going to be confirmed.

Whether or not these are the right scenarios, or cover all possible scenarios, isn't really the point of this example. The point is that the test cases for this feature are written on the back of the card, in support of the information about the feature, and before the feature is developed.

Generally speaking, there is a very fine line between a requirements scenario and a test case, so it isn't necessary to capture too much detail on the front of the card and clutter it up. The card in its entirety represents the requirements for the feature; whether captured in the Conversation section or the Confirmation section.

Even the description of the user story in the Card section carries some important information. In this case, there is a pre-condition (the user must be registered) and a post-condition (the user can access subscriber-only content). All of the card must be read to get the whole story.

Importantly, the User Story is expressed in business language, and in a micro, more easily digestible, information-packed format.

'INVEST' In Good User Stories

User Stories are certainly an easy concept. But what makes a good User Story? That's a bit of an open question. I'm sure everyone has a different opinion of what good looks like. But there are certainly some common characteristics of a good User Story.

A common and simple way to remember and assess whether or not a User Story is well formed is the INVEST acronym. A good User Story should be:

Independent
Negotiable
Valuable
Estimable
Small
Testable

Personally I'm not really a big fan of management acronyms - they can be a bit cheesy. But I do like this one. I think it's very helpful for people new to writing User Stories to remember and assess what makes a good one, particularly as User Stories are such an open format.

In the following pages, I explain each of these attributes in more detail...

User Stories Should Be *Independent*

The 'I' in 'INVEST' stands for Independent. Ideally a User Story would be as small as possible, without making it too dependent on other Stories.

Earlier I showed you an example of a User Story. In the next few pages, I'm going to use the 'INVEST' acronym to assess whether or not this example is any good?

So, first, let's take a look at whether it's Independent? Personally I see a problem already. In my example of a user login story, I included a link for 'Forgotten Password', but this is actually a separate story that isn't covered on the card.

When I did this example, I deliberately didn't include the forgotten password feature, in order to keep the story small and fit it on the card. But I did put the forgotten password link on as a reminder of the related story.

If a developer implemented this story as per the card, the forgotten password feature would be a broken link until the related story was implemented. If the Sprint or iteration had finished with the Login story completed and not the Forgotten Password story, the product would not be shippable.

Therefore this is not a good example in terms of being Independent.

If, however, I had left the link off of this story, and included it on the Forgotten Password story instead, the Login story could have been implemented in its entirety without reliance on other features that may or may not be completed.

So, unfortunately for me, I've failed on the first test! My example User Story is not Independent and the 'INVEST' acronym would have helped me spot that straight away. I wonder how I'll do on the other points...

User Stories Should Be *Negotiable*

The 'N' in 'INVEST' stands for Negotiable. User Stories are not a contract. They are not meant to be precise, detailed specifications of a feature. They should not be fixed in stone.

A User Story is a reminder. A reminder to have a conversation about a feature. A reminder to collaborate in order to understand the details just in time for the feature to be developed. Notes can be made on the User Story as details are captured and clarified.

A User Story should have sufficient information to capture the essence of a feature without requiring too much collaboration for the basics. However, a User Story should not contain too much detail. Too much information can imply that the User Story is complete and precise.

So much more information can be gained from a conversation because of the rich, two-way nature of a verbal exchange. Too much information on a User Story can cause people not to collaborate, believing they already know everything they need to. Then you lose out. You lose out on the advantages of combining a written reminder with a verbal, face to face communication.

One of my 10 key principles of agile development is that 'agile requirements are barely sufficient'. Sufficient. But barely. No more information than is necessary to proceed with development and testing with reasonable efficiency.

Sometimes a requirement may have been 'specified' in a particular way, and a developer finds that it's awkward to implement. Or that there's an easier alternative. In these cases, a small compromise, or a slight change in approach to the feature, can simplify and speed up the implementation. User Stories should be Negotiable, so no time is wasted when the user or customer's goals can be met an easier way.

So, using the 'INVEST' acronym, how does my recent example of a User Story look in terms of being Negotiable?

Perhaps it's a bit detailed? It implies a particular design approach to the functionality behind the button. Although this is really just a note about a key decision for the design approach that should be adopted; there is no detail on the design of the feature itself.

The visual approach implies a specific screen layout, although it's meant to be a wireframe rather than a screen shot. Personally speaking, as long as people treat it as Negotiable, I think a picture is worth a thousand words and this is well worthwhile.

This example is possibly as detailed as a User Story should really need to get. Certainly I wouldn't expect to see every User Story as detailed as this. Many User Stories could probably be described with less detail, and still be (barely) sufficient.

User Stories Should Be *Valuable*

The 'V' in 'INVEST' stands for Valuable.

It is often said by people in the agile community that User Stories should be of value to the user. Whilst that is mostly true, some User Stories are not of value to the user, but rather of value to the customer or owner of the system.

Therefore it is more accurate to say that, "User Stories should be of value to the user, or owner, of the solution".

A good example of this is advertising space on a public web site. Ads can be of value to the user, if they are highly relevant and positioned in a place sensitive to the user experience. For example on Google. On the other hand, very often the ads on a web site are of little value to the user and interfere with content, creating a poor user experience. Of course I would never advocate creating a poor user experience, but regardless of the debate about value to the user, they are certainly of value to the owner of the solution.

User Stories should be focused on features - not tasks. And written in business language. Doing so will enable business people to understand and prioritise the User Stories.

For example, a User Story to 'comply with OWASP security standards' should be written something like this: 'As a user, I want my data to be secure, so I can use the system without my personal information being misused'.

This brings me to the question of non-functional User Stories that in effect span all other User Stories. For example the above story about security, or maybe a user story about the solution's performance. These can be captured as User Stories to ensure the requirement is not lost. But actually these requirements are possibly better served by writing a series of standard Confirmations to be applied to all User Stories.

So let's take a look at my recent example of a User Story in terms of being Valuable to the user or owner of the solution?

An agile consultant saw this example and said it was not a good example because logging in to the solution is of no value to the user.

But in this case I disagree.

It is of value to the user, because only by logging in can they gain access to features and content that are available to subscribers only. And it's also of value to the owner, as it prevents people from accessing premium areas of the solution unless they have paid to subscribe.

Of course, we are both right really. Until the other features are implemented, this story does have limited value. However the trick is to balance this with keeping them small.

User Stories Should Be *Estimable*

The 'E' in 'INVEST' stands for Estimable. User Stories should be possible to estimate.

If you follow the other aspects of the 'INVEST' acronym, chances are they will be. So what are the potential barriers to a User Story being estimable?

Too big?
Maybe the story is too big? In this case, simply break it down into multiple User Stories, until it is more reasonable to estimate.

Not enough information, or requires domain knowledge
Maybe there is not enough information, the story is too vague, or requires domain knowledge to properly understand what is meant? In this case, there are 2 aspects of the Scrum agile development method that help with this issue...

Firstly, in Sprint Planning, discuss the requirement as a team with the Product Owner and/or user representative. Do not attempt to estimate it until you feel you have clarified it enough to really understand the requirement. Capture some further information or notes on the User Story Card.

Secondly, break the requirement down into tasks; ideally tasks of less than one day. Do this as a team. Breaking the requirement down will obviously help to estimate it. Breaking the requirement down into tasks of less than one day will make each task more predictable and the estimate is likely to be more accurate as a result.

Doing this in Sprint Planning just in time, just before a Sprint, and involving the whole team, will help to ensure that everyone on the team understands the requirements. And, importantly, the information will still be fresh when the feature is being developed and tested.

New technology or not enough knowledge in the team
Another potential barrier is that the product or specific User Story may involve new technologies that the team has not worked with before. First this means the team will be less productive and may not be able to rely on their past experiences. Second it means the team simply may not know how to implement it.

In this case, someone in the team needs to be able to complete a brief research task before the User Story is estimated. This research needs to be time-boxed and they need to do only enough research and/or prototyping to estimate the work more reliably. This should ideally be done during the Sprint Planning cycle if at all possible, or if it's going to take longer should be done early in the Sprint or in the Sprint before, before the story is committed in the Sprint Backlog.

It's worth having a few User Stories in reserve, either as stretch tasks or in case the research determines the story cannot be accommodated in the current Sprint. In Extreme Programming, this research task is called a 'spike'.

So, now let's look at my recent example of a User Story and see whether or not it feels like it's Estimable?

It's certainly not too big. It's very familiar and doesn't require any domain knowledge. We all know how to log in to systems and know what to expect. I don't think it's vague. In fact, I think it contains quite a lot of information for such a small card. Technically it's straightforward. And in our case it was being developed in familiar technology. So I'd say this example is dead easy to estimate, so the story in this respect is good.

User Stories Should Be *Small*

The 'S' in 'INVEST' stands for Small. User Stories should be small.

Not too small. But certainly not too big. So what is the right size for a good User Story?

First of all, let's get one thing straight. This statement is slightly misleading. More accurately, it should read: "User Stories should be Small, by the time you plan to include them in a Sprint".

Because until you come to Sprint Planning - until you're ready to include the feature in the next iteration - User Stories can be big. In fact, they can be huge. Humongous even!

It's completely reasonable for User Stories that are further down the Product Backlog to be rather large and fuzzy. As long as they are broken down before it's time to work on them, that's fine. They are still effective placeholders.

So it's okay to have a User Story further down the backlog like: "As a user, I want a new system, because the old one no longer meets my needs".

These big User Stories are known as Epics. In fact this example is huge, even for an epic.

Anyway, back to the point in hand. What's a good size for User Stories when they are ready to be developed?

Let's take my recent example of a User Story. This could have been: "As a user, I want to register, log in and manage my details online". But I think that's too big to be a good User Story. Perhaps it started life like that, as an epic, further down the backlog. That would be fine. But at the time of Sprint Planning, a story like this should be broken down.

So let's say it's broken down into 3 stories: register, login, and manage details. The login story could potentially be broken down further, into another 3 stories, for example: login, forgotten password, remember me. In my opinion that's still a nice size. The stories are very focused. Small. But still each story is still functional and fulfills its own purpose. And they're still fairly Independent.

Now let's say the login story is broken down even further. For example: "As a user, I want to enter my user id", "As a user, I want to enter my password", "As a user I want to push the login button", "As a user, I want a clear error message when my login fails", etc. Then I'd say it's gone too far. These stories are too detailed. At this level, the Value of each story to the user is really not there, and even a small project would end up with hundreds of stories and be very hard to manage.

In the end, there's really no right or wrong here - you need to do what feels right for you and your team. Nevertheless, I hope my comments offer some useful guidance, even if it's just as a starting point for your team to debate.

User Stories Should Be *Testable*

The 'T' in 'INVEST' stands for Testable.

The most common forms of User Story that are not testable are big User Stories, known as Epics.

An Epic can be a User Story that really comprises multiple User Stories. Or perhaps an Epic can also be a User Story that is very complex.

An example from a previous job might be something like: "As a user, I want to calculate the cost of repairing a crashed car". This is really an Epic and is not really Testable.

Let's take my recent example of a User Story to see if it's Testable?

First of all, it's small and fairly independent, which makes it inherently more testable to start with. This is a simple example so it should be easy to test. The scenarios are: Successful login, Failed login (user id), Failed login (password), Failed login (expired account), Failed login (authentication system unavailable), Remember me (if login successful and this is ticked).

Importantly, identify the tests up-front, before the User Story is implemented. If developers know how the User Story will be tested, maybe they will write it to pass?

User Stories Versus Use Cases

You may be familiar with Use Cases, another method for capturing requirements. When I first used Use Cases, I loved them.

I loved the fact they gave such a clear description of a feature, and the fact that each Use Case could stand alone. They made it really easy to move cards representing the Use Cases around the whiteboard, as a way of managing progress.

But I also found Use Cases a little complicated sometimes. When you look closely, they're not that complicated really, but they tend to need an Analyst to write them, because they have a very particular structure. And in my experience they tend to be a bit off-putting for end users or business people. I think this is partly because they use quite a bit of jargon, and particularly when faced with a lot of them, all up-front, to be signed off and used against them in a change control process later!

So when I came across User Stories, I loved them even more. They seemed to offer all the things I loved about Use Cases, but in a simpler, lighter and easier-to-use format. They're easier to write. And they're much easier for end users or business people to work with.

Having said that, User Stories leave out a lot of important details. They leave these details out deliberately, relying on a conversation with the product owner to clarify the details at the time of development. They rely on this collaboration. Developing small increments, getting feedback and iterating, rather than having more detailed documentation up-front. Without this collaboration, I agree, User Stories could be problematic.

Having said that, if the product owner won't collaborate on User Stories throughout development, why would they collaborate on Use Cases during the analysis? In the end, whichever approach you prefer, active user involvement is imperative!

That's Not A User Story, That's An Epic!

Earlier on I mentioned the concept of Epics.

When putting User Stories onto a Product Backlog (or feature list), you shouldn't feel compelled to break everything down until the features are nearing development.

Further down the Product Backlog, it's fine for items to be fairly fuzzy. It's also fine for items further down the backlog to be whole projects - large, high-level items that are not so much User Stories but more like Epics!

As an item nears development, the item should be broken down further. And as it nears development, the item on the backlog should be defined in sufficient detail that the team can reasonably estimate its size and break it into tasks. Until that time, however, it's just really a placeholder. A reminder for prioritisation and high-level estimating. That's all.

For some people, particularly those used to a more traditional project approach, used to detailed specifications up-front, this can potentially feel very uncomfortable. It shouldn't.

The logic here is simple. There is little point defining a feature (or set of features) in detail if it may never reach the top of the priorities. The other aspect of this logic is that you tend to know more about your requirements, constraints, etc as time goes by. And things change. People come and go. Sometimes the team has changed significantly since the original requirements emerged, so information can be lost or now wrong if it is captured too early.

Therefore it makes business sense to defer details until they are needed, and just capture reminders as Epics in the meantime.

There is a saying in agile, "Make decisions at the last responsible moment". Epics on the backlog are a great example of this. The later you make the decision, the more information you will have about your situation and the better your decision is therefore likely to be. Making decisions too late (or not making them at all), however, is also problematic of course. Hence the important point being 'the last *responsible* moment'.

User Story Themes

Agile software development teams often use User Stories as a simple and concise way to express user requirements. Ideally these User Stories are broken down as small as possible, whilst also trying to minimise dependencies.

Naturally, though, as you break User Stories down smaller, they become increasingly inter-dependent. Like most things in software development, it's a balancing act.

Break the User Stories down as small as possible. But stop breaking them down when it becomes onerous or pointless to do so. When a User Story can be delivered (done) in less than 1 or 2 days, I think there is little point breaking it down any further.

Use the concept of Themes to categorise these related User Stories under one label and keep them together.

You could physically keep the cards together by paper-clipping them to each other. Or you could put a card representing the Theme on the left of your whiteboard, and keep related User Stories on the same row as the Theme as they move across the board.

Assigning Themes to the User Stories in your Product Backlog can help you to see emerging themes, which with a loose set of User Stories you may not have noticed. When you see emerging themes for your next Sprint or two, this can help to give extra clarity to the team and business about the Sprint Goals for the next period of development.

This is a useful thing to do. It gives you more of a message for the Sprint. It's actually about something, rather than a random collection of high value but unrelated stories. It could tell you that you're focusing a high percentage of your Sprint on features x and y, when at a macro level your priorities are really elsewhere, for example.

It also helps when priorities are set top-down. For example, let's say we make the commercial decision that for the next few sprints SEO will be a top priority. You can quickly grab all the User Stories with the SEO Theme and give them priority.

Of course it's fine for a Sprint to include items that are not part of the overall Theme. The theme is simply the main area of focus, not necessarily the sole area of focus.

There is sometimes a danger with agile software development that everything is broken down so small and incremental that everything becomes a bit too tactical, and there is either no direction or at least the direction is not apparent.

It's important to keep a higher level Release Plan, or a Product Roadmap, so the Sprints do take the product in a certain direction, and so the team can see what that direction is. Because no Sprint is an island!

You can use the concept of Themes as a simple way to sketch out broad priorities on the Product Roadmap, showing the key areas of focus over time.

Writing Good User Stories

Here is a quick summary of the key points about User Stories…

User Stories are a simple way of capturing user requirements throughout a project just in time to be developed - an alternative to writing lengthy requirements specifications all up-front.

As a guide for people writing User Stories, they follow this basic construct:

As a [user role], I want to [goal], so I can [reason]

This helps to ensure that the requirement is captured at a high level, is feature oriented and covers who, what and why.

As well as capturing User Stories in the above format on the Product Backlog, User Stories should be written on a card when it's time to develop them.

The card comprises 3 parts:
- **Card** ("as a user, I want…, so I can…")
- **Conversation** (notes or small wireframe to remind people about the feature)
- **Confirmations** (the tests that will show the feature is complete)

Ultimately, User Stories should be small. But when they're first entered on the Product Backlog, when they're quite a way from being developed, they can start out large and fuzzy. While they are in this state, they are known as Epics.

Software requirements are a communication problem. We accept that there is no perfect solution. User Stories seek to find a balance between written and verbal requirements, relying on close collaboration between team members to clarify details near the time of development.

The INVEST acronym can help you to remember and assess what makes a good User Story. User Stories should be:

- Independent
- Negotiable
- Valuable
- Estimable
- Small
- Testable

Agile Estimating

Agile Estimating: The Secret To Delivering On Time

For decades, delivering on time has been the holy grail of software development.

I've been doing agile software development for some years now. I've seen many benefits, but one of the most remarkable things of all, is how so many teams can quickly get good at delivering on time. It's the art - or science - of predicting what can be delivered in a given timeframe, even if the same team was hopeless at estimating before!

This, for me, is one of the most compelling reasons to do agile development. In summary, here is the secret:

- Estimate features, rather than tasks.
- Keep your estimates high-level intuitive guesses (don't analyse the details).
- Estimate in points to indicate the relative size of each feature.
- Use a number sequence like Fibonacci. Fibonacci numbers get less precise as they get bigger, which builds a natural distribution curve into your estimates.
- Estimate as a team. Consider playing Planning Poker to facilitate this.
- At the end of your Sprint (or iteration), score the points for all features you managed to deliver. Only score points for features 100% complete, tested and potentially shippable. This is your Velocity. Count zero for incomplete features, even if they are very close to completion.
- Track your Velocity over time on a graph. You can also track your Predictability, i.e. the number of points delivered as a percentage of the number of points committed to at the start of the Sprint.
- At the start of each Sprint, look back at your Velocity for recent Sprints to decide how much to commit to for the coming Sprint.

- Resist the urge to try to reconcile points with hours or days.
- Commit to the Sprint as a team.

Like most great things in life, it's actually very simple. That's really the beauty of it. It seems a bit abstract, so many people might be reluctant to give it a try. I urge you to try it.

You'll need to give it several Sprints before you pass judgement on it. You will find your Velocity bounces all over the place for the first 3-4 Sprints. But then it will settle down, as your team discovers its norm.

Trust me, it works. I have seen it work in many different teams, time and time again. It's a statistical approach to estimating. And statistically, if you estimate with relativity, everything is average in the end.

What Is The Point In Estimating?

Estimating in points is a common technique used by agile development teams. This approach has a few distinct advantages over estimating in physical units of time.

1. Estimating is very quick because it's an intuitive estimate of a feature's size.

2. An estimate in points indicates a feature's size relative to another, and does not give the illusion of being precise.

3. Over time, and using consistent iterations (e.g. 2-week sprints), you get a strong feel for how many points a team can deliver in an iteration. Even if a team is bad at estimating, as long as they're consistently bad, this makes a team's commitments self-correcting.

Some agile teams use Fibonacci numbers to do this. Fibonacci numbers are a sequence where each number is the sum of the previous two, i.e.

1, 2, 3, 5, 8, 13, 21 ...

Using Fibonacci adds an element of science to the concept of estimating using points, adding the laws of distribution as a dimension.

Estimating in Points Seems a Bit Stupid!

To be honest, I didn't understand the concept of estimating in Points when we first adopted agile. Actually, I thought it sounded a bit stupid! But I get it now, and it makes a lot of sense.

Developers are more inclined to give a relative estimate in points based on minimal information about a feature, whereas to estimate in days implies precision and can be a barrier to getting someone to commit to how big it is.

But the key thing about estimating in points is actually about how a team's estimating is self-correcting. Even if they are bad at it.

Let me give you some examples...

Let's say your team estimates they can complete 100 Points in a Sprint. Actually, they over-estimated because they're naturally cautious, and in practice you find they deliver 150 Points. Great news! Next Sprint you bring 150 Points into Sprint Planning. Imagine that in hours. Imagine your team's response when you say they tend to be cautious, so your going to plan on them doing 7.5 days a week! Not going to go down too well I suspect.

Now look at it the other way round. The team again estimates 100 Points but actually achieves only 50. In this case the team is over-optimistic and let's say they consistently under-estimate, causing late delivery or delivery of reduced scope. You adjust accordingly and bring only 50 Points into the Sprint, because you know that's what they can typically achieve. They start to deliver on time and the business unit or customer is happy because you're meeting expectations. Now imagine this in days. You tell the customer or business you're only going to plan on the team doing 2.5 days a week because you know they tend to under-estimate, or you use negative statements like you're planning on 50% productivity or utilisation. Not going to go down well either!

Using Points makes the unit of estimation abstract, which makes it easier to commit to, and easier to adjust your commitments to.

Of course on a project, making this adjustment could mean you won't be able to deliver everything you planned to in the original timescales. Agile - and estimating in points - doesn't solve that. But it will highlight it early, while there's still time to do something about it.

And the self-correcting nature of estimating in points will help you to meet expectations more consistently.

Agile Estimating in Scrum -
Why Estimate Twice?

In the earlier chapter about "How to Implement Scrum in 10 Easy Steps", I refer to two stages of estimating:

- Step 2 is how to estimate your Product Backlog.
- Step 4 is estimating tasks in Sprint Planning.

Someone recently asked me a very good question - why estimate twice? I thought it would be worth addressing this question here...

The idea is that the first estimate, in points, is a high level estimate of everything on the Product Backlog.

At the time of estimating in points, the team has very little detail on what the requirements really are or what the feature has to do. They may be estimating from a simple heading or description.

This high level estimate helps with medium term planning (Release Planning) and helps the Product Owner to prioritise everything with some sense of how big the features are relative to each other.

Later, these points are used to calculate Velocity, which means the team get statistically better at predicting what they can achieve from very quick high-level estimates, which is obviously very useful.

The second estimate is meant to be a detailed estimate for only those things that are included in the next Sprint.

Here, the team has the opportunity to potentially see some prior analysis of the requirements, to discuss the feature with the product owner and any other stakeholders, and to discuss the technical implications as a team.

At this stage, the team is in a much better position to break the feature down into tasks and estimate in hours or days.

At this stage, it is also possible to take account of the team's actual capacity at that time - i.e. how many team members available for the sprint, any other commitments, holidays, etc. With this information, the team should be able to plan the next Sprint reasonably accurately.

I have found that some teams like the second Sprint Planning estimates in hours or days, and other teams can do without them.

The teams that do without still have the Sprint Planning meeting, which they still use it to discuss the requirements and technical design of the features in the next sprint, but they don't bother trying to break the features into tasks and estimate them in hours because they found invariably they were wrong anyway so it was a waste of everyone's time. Teams that are more accurate at estimating may be the ones that find it most useful for planning.

The teams that drop the task-based estimates rely entirely on their historic Velocity (in points) to decide how much to commit to in each sprint, so they let the statistics take care of it. If they have a lot of absence, or a team member missing, for any one Sprint, they simply commit to a slightly lower Velocity.

Personally I favour this approach. It's nice and simple and in my experience the statistical approach to estimating is just as accurate as the analytical approach, if not more so. The trouble with estimating analytically is that you only estimate what you can think of, and inevitably you can't really think of everything. Even if you think you can.

One thing I can say for sure, though, is that the Sprint Planning meeting is still exceptionally useful for the team to discuss the next Sprint together, whether you break down the tasks and estimate them or not.

To Estimate or Not To Estimate?
That is the Question!

Lean software development shares many of the key principles of agile software development.

One of the key aspects of lean development is all about identifying and eliminating waste from the development process. One of the most hotly debated aspects of this is estimating. It clearly doesn't contribute to the end product itself, but is estimating really waste? Or does it really add value to the process?

The answer? I guess it really is a matter of opinion. My personal answer - like most things in life, I think it depends!

If you're working on high priority bugs, in severity order, and they must be fixed, estimating how long they will take provides little value, except to help manage expectations about when the bugs might be gone, which may or may not be useful depending on your circumstances.

On the other hand, if you need to create a business case in order to secure funding for a special project, or you need to commit to a deadline to fit in with other dependencies like a launch date, estimating is clearly necessary, whether it adds value to the end product or not.

I think actually that's really the wrong question though. Clearly there are many scenarios in business where you do need to estimate when something might be done. But you may not need to estimate the size of each feature or the effort of each task in order to predict a delivery date.

Lean methods include the idea of 'cycle time'. With a large enough sample size, keeping track of the average time per feature, or cycle time, could potentially be a reliable way of predicting how long something might take, without actually estimating it.

My concern about this approach is that, statistically, all items must be as near as possible to average to achieve any level of predictability on a single piece of work. I'm sure on a large project, everything averages out. By definition it must do!

But on smaller pieces of work, where you're working to short timescales, any feature that is higher than average gets delivered later than expected. And that can cause problems. That's why I personally favour estimating in points, rather than simply tracking cycle time.

Planning Poker

Planning Poker is an estimating technique used by many agile software development teams. Like many agile development techniques, Planning Poker is very simple. Simple, but effective.

First of all, agile teams should ideally estimate together. As a team. If the team is big, and people are working on different products, it's okay to split the team into smaller groups. But estimates should still be done in groups.

The logic behind this is simple. Each person in the team has different experience. When you get the input of multiple people, you multiply the experience applied to the problem.
The benefit of doing this is based on the wisdom of crowds. You get the benefit of the team's collective intelligence.

In addition, you are likely to generate more ideas. Ideas about different ways of solving the problem. Ideas about how to design the solution. And ideas about obstacles that might be encountered.

All this leads to better estimating. And perhaps more importantly, better solutions.

Here's how it works...

First of all, agree an estimating approach. For instance, many agile teams estimate in points, perhaps using the Fibonacci numbering sequence. Others use T-shirt sizes or some other abstract numbering system. Estimating in an abstract form has several benefits. The key thing is to estimate each item's relative size, compared to other items.

Then, prepare cards with the numbers on. You can buy Fibonacci Planning Poker cards, or make your own. Alternatively you can just ask people to write the numbers you'll be using on post-it notes or hold their fingers up.

The actual process of Planning Poker is then to discuss each feature in turn, clarifying requirements and asking questions that help to understand how it might be designed. When questions about a feature have run out, or are no longer materially important to the size, each member of the team indicates they are ready to give their estimate.

Then, on the count of three, the whole team reveals their estimate by showing the appropriate card, all at the same time.

As I mentioned earlier, each member of the team has different experience. So it's very unlikely that everyone will come up with the same answer. Maybe someone saw issues and risks that others did not. Maybe someone else thought of an easier solution. The team uses this difference of opinion as the basis for discussion, sharing ideas and concerns.

Following the discussion, the whole team re-votes. This process continues until there's only a small difference, or ideally until the team has agreed on the size of the feature.

Then the team moves on to the next feature, doing the same again.

And that's it! Planning Poker is a very simple but powerful technique, designed to extract the collective wisdom of the team, without any individual team members having an over-bearing influence.

Agile Estimating In A Nutshell

Here is a summary of the key aspects of agile estimating...

Product Backlog
The Product Backlog is a feature list. Or a list of User Stories if that's your approach. Either way, it is a simple list of things that are of value to a user - not technical tasks - and they are written in business language, so they can be prioritised by the Product Owner. There are no details about each feature until it is ready to be developed, just a basic description and maybe a few notes if applicable.

'Points Make Sizes'
Each item on the Product Backlog is given a points value to represent its size. Size is an intuitive mixture of effort and complexity. It's meant to represent how big it feels.

Fibonacci
I like to use the Fibonacci number sequence for the points values. Fibonacci goes 1, 2, 3, 5, 8, 13 - where each number is the sum of the previous two. This builds a natural distribution curve into the estimates. The bigger something's size, the less precise the estimate can be, which is reflected in the widening range between the numbers as they get bigger.

Relative Estimating
Points are an abstract number. They do not convert to a unit of time. They are simply a relative indication of size. In other words, a 2 is about twice the size of a 1. A 5 is bigger than a 3, but smaller than an 8. Developers find it hard to estimate accurately in hours or days when they don't yet know the details of the requirements and what the solution involves. But it's easier to compare the size of two features relative to each other.

Estimate as a Team
The points should be assigned to each backlog item as a team. The collective intelligence - or wisdom of crowds - is an important way

to apply multiple people's experience to the estimate. If you have a very big team, you can split up so it's quicker to do this, but the estimating groups should ideally involve at least 3 people, so you don't just get two opposing opinions.

Planning Poker

Planning Poker is a fun technique to facilitate rapid estimating as a team. The team discusses a feature verbally to understand more about what it entails and how it might be done. Each team member writes what they think its size is (in points) on a card. All team members reveal their card at the same time. Differences in opinion are used to provoke further discussion. Maybe one person saw risks and complexity that others didn't. Maybe another person saw a simpler solution. The team re-votes until there is a consensus, then moves on to the next item.

Done Means Done!

During the Sprint, or iteration, the team only counts something as done when it is completely done, i.e. tested and signed off by the Product Owner. At that time, and only at that time, the team scores the points for the item.

Burndown

The team shows its commitment and daily progress on a graph, so it is measurable and visible at a glance. This is called a Burndown Chart. The burndown shows the total number of points committed to, depreciating over time to the end of the Sprint. This is the target line. It also shows the actual number of points scored each day - i.e. the sum of points for all items that are 100% done and signed off so far. The team plots this each day before their daily stand-up meeting.   When the actual line is above the target line, the team is behind. When it's below, they're ahead.

Velocity

At the end of the Sprint, the team's score is called their Velocity. The team tracks its Velocity over time. This allows the team to see if it's improving. Of course at some point it will stabilise, if the team is stable. If not, this is an issue in itself. When Velocity is relatively stable - in my experience that will be after 3 or 4 Sprints - it can be reliably used to decide how much (i.e. how many points) the team should commit to in the next Sprint.

Reliability / Predictability
As a result, the team can measure how reliable - or how predictable - they are. The metric for this is Velocity (points scored) as a percentage of points planned. As Velocity stabilises, the team's Reliability will get better, and the team will be better at predicting what they can deliver. Ironically, the team doesn't need to get better at estimating to get better at delivering on their commitments. Even if they are terrible at estimating, as long as they are consistently terrible, with this method they will still get better at predicting what they can deliver.

Points Versus Time
One of the benefits of points is that it does not relate to time. Resist the temptation to convert it. If a team plans on 100 points and delivers 50, can you imagine telling your stakeholders that you are only planning future Sprints for half the team's time. If a team commits to 100 points and delivers 150, imagine telling the team you're planning on doing 60 hours each per week. It just doesn't work. Points are not a measure of time. They are abstract, relative sizes, and a measure of how much can be delivered. That's why it works. It works because the team can adjust its commitment based on what its track record shows it can usually deliver.

Productivity
This does not measure a team's productivity. Velocity does tell you if a team is getting more or less productive. But you can't really use Velocity to compare the productivity of two teams, as their circumstances are different. And you can't use it to determine whether a team's Velocity is as high as it should be. For this, you still need to use your judgement, based on previous experience and taking into account many subjective factors.

Playing the System

Using these two metrics - Velocity and Reliability/Predictability - it's hard to cheat the system. If a team commits low, they achieve Reliability but Velocity goes down. If a team commits too high, their Velocity goes up but their Reliability goes down. This is like the balanced scorecard concept. The metrics are deliberately measuring opposing things, so they can't easily be played.

Agile Testing

Test Driven Development

XP (Extreme Programming) advocates Test Driven Development, where automated unit tests are written before the code. Radical, huh?

If you think about it, it makes complete sense. Assuming you are planning to write automated unit tests anyway, it's no more effort than writing them later. And the big advantage of writing them first?

If you know how you're going to test it, you write the code to pass first time! Simple really. Simple but inspired.

Developers Can't Test For Toffee!

In the more traditional world of managing software development projects, it is widely acknowledged that developers can't test for toffee!

Yet agile development methods increasingly seem to require or imply that all people in the project team should test, including developers.

So, first of all, why is it that developers can't test? Are we to believe that these highly intelligent individuals somehow don't have what it takes to test? Of course not.

The trouble is simply this: Good developers build their code to handle every scenario they can think of. If they're really good developers, they write automated unit tests to test everything they've built. And if they're really good developers, they even do this up-front so everything is designed and built to pass first time.

But still it's not enough.

For developers only build (and therefore test) everything they can think of. And testers, partly due to their nature and partly due to the fact they're not buried in the detail of implementing the code, are able to think up scenarios that the developer didn't think of. And that's the problem.

So what do we do in agile development, where everyone might be expected to test?

My answer is this. Wherever possible, do include at least one dedicated tester within the agile development team. If the tester is not able to test everything personally because there are more developers than the tester can handle, have the tester take a special QA role, including the following activities:

- Identify the test strategy and test scenarios

- Ensure the appropriate test environments are in place and controlled

- Write the test cases/story confirmations - ideally up-front but on a just-in-time basis per feature

- Review the developers' automated unit tests, to avoid re-testing the same things later and to QA the scope of the tests

- Execute some of the most important test cases personally, particularly where there is higher complexity or risk, less clarity or where more attention to detail is required

- Coordinate the test efforts of others (including developers), so one person knows what tests have been executed, what areas have been tested, their status at any time, and the issues logged against them

- Manage the bug log to ensure issues are logged clearly and prioritised consistently

- Liaise with customers and/or business users to organise acceptance testing and advise on approach

- Ensure that each developer's code is tested by someone other than the person that wrote it, even if it's another developer

In my experience, there is real business value in having tester expertise for this quality management / quality assurance role, even in a situation where there aren't enough testers to go round. In an agile development environment, the emphasis of a tester's role is more on QA than it is on just testing per se.

Why Agile Testers Should Be In At The Start

In my experience, some people implement agile principles within the development team itself, but leave other key roles (for instance business users or testers) out of, or on the fringes, of the agile team.

Earlier I wrote that active user involvement is imperative in agile development for a wide variety of reasons. It's just as important for the agile team to include all roles required to ensure that each feature is actually complete (that is 100% complete) at the end of each iteration or Sprint.

In particular it's a good idea to include testers from the outset, and especially in planning, because:

- Testers tend to be exceptionally good at clarifying requirements and identifying alternative scenarios. Doing this thinking at the requirements clarification and planning stage improves the quality of estimates given for the work, and therefore increases the chances of successfully delivering in the timescales.

- When more is known about the test approach up-front, developers are more inclined to write their code to pass.

- Testers that are involved in requirements clarification and planning first-hand will have a much better understanding of what's needed and how it is being implemented, enabling them to do a better job of testing. In the absence of a lengthy specification, this is essential in agile development projects to allow a tester to do their job effectively.

- And testing must be completed within each Sprint for completed features to be 100% done, i.e. production ready.

For all of these reasons, testers really need to be on the project team from the very beginning.

Agile Testing Versus Waterfall Test Phases

I have recently been asked by a tester how agile testing compares to the various test phases in more traditional, waterfall development projects.

For instance, after the code has been unit tested, are there several testing phases, such as system, integration and regression testing?

Although these layers of testing do exist in agile projects, agile testing is integrated throughout the lifecycle, with each feature being fully tested as it's developed, rather than doing most testing at the end of all the development.

Here's how traditional test phases typically fit in with an agile testing approach:

- Unit testing is still completed by developers as usual, but ideally there's a much stronger emphasis on automated testing at the code/unit level.

- In Extreme Programming (XP), there is also a strong emphasis on test driven development, which is the practice of writing tests before writing code. This can start simply with tests (or 'confirmations') being identified when a 'user story' is written, and can go as far as actually writing automated unit tests before writing any code.

- System testing and integration testing are rolled together. As there is at least a daily build, and ideally continuous integration, features can be tested as they are developed, in an integrated environment. As per waterfall, this stage of testing is ideally carried out by professional testers, as we all know developers can't test for toffee! Importantly, though, each feature is tested as it's developed, not at the end of the Sprint or iteration, and certainly not at the end of the project.

- Towards the end of each Sprint, when all features for the iteration have been completed (i.e. developed and tested in an integrated environment), there needs to be time for a short regression test before releasing the software. Regression testing should be short because automated, test driven development, with features tested continuously in an integrated environment, should not result in many surprises. Hopefully it should be more like a 'road test'.

- Finally, on a very large project, where a release must practically span multiple sprints to be of any value, a 'stabilisation' sprint may be worthwhile to make sure everything is okay before release. This should, however, be a short duration and the need for a stabilisation sprint should be avoided if at all possible, by trying to deliver releasable quality in each and every sprint along the way. If it is required, this sprint should be all about reducing any defects prior to launch, and the scope of development should at that time be frozen.

That's a very quick summary of how traditional test phases fit in with an agile testing approach. In many ways it's common sense, although it's not always easy to achieve.

The Changing Role of Testers

In my opinion, the most challenging role to adapt to agile development is the role of tester.

That's because agile development contradicts so many things that many testers have been taught is 'best practice'.

Testers might typically have gone through some recognised training such as ISEB certification. ISEB testing qualifications, for example, specifically acknowledge iterative-incremental development models, including agile methods.

However, many testers would have undertaken their training, or gained their experience, when the waterfall model was more prevalent. And consequently would have potentially spent years practicing what is known as the V-model. With the V-model, system testing correlates directly to the system's specification, and testing is conducted when the software is completed.

Put simply, a tester's life in traditional development methods was reasonably straight-forward. Give a tester a spec and a finished piece of software, and they can check it works as specified.

Forget whether what was specified was really what the user wanted, or whether all the requirements were adequately captured, if it meets the spec, the quality is supposedly good.

With agile development methods, a tester's life is rather more complicated.

First of all, there are no big documents specifying every detail of the requirements and functionality for them to test against. Only small pieces of documentation per feature and details often captured verbally through collaboration.

Secondly, the software is tested early and throughout the lifecycle while it is still being developed. In other words, it's a moving target.

Put like that, agile testing can be a real challenge.

Add to that the idea of writing test cases up-front, before the software is developed, so acceptance tests form part of the requirements analysis.

Add to that the idea that some tests will be automated at code level and implemented by developers.

Add to that a much greater emphasis on automated regression testing due to the fact that feature-level testing has been completed while the code was still being developed.

To cope with such demands, an agile tester's role must change.

Some of the key differences I've observed are as follows:

- With User Stories, there is little difference between a requirements scenario and a test case. Some requirements are implied from the test cases.

- If test cases are written up-front, there's a fine line between requirements analysis and test analysis.

- A Business Analyst may have special skills in workshop facilitation, interviewing, gathering business requirements, etc. But, regarding functional analysis, tester and analyst roles start to converge.

- If unit tests are automated, a tester needs to work with developers to ensure that the tests are complete and appropriate, and that all important scenarios have been identified.

- Testers need to avoid duplicating tests that have already been adequately unit tested when they and others come to system test the features.

- Automated regression tests need to be written and maintained.

- The tester's involvement is increasingly important throughout the entire lifecycle of the development, not just in the latter stages of development.

The role of an agile tester is more aptly described as Test Analyst, and is more of a general QA role for the team, not necessarily the person who executes all the tests.

Putting the *Analyst* into Test Analyst

For years, I've given Software Testers in my teams the official job title of Test Analyst, or something along those lines. Yet (informally) I've always referred to them as Testers. Only in more recent years - and especially since adopting agile methods and User Stories - have I really discovered how to put the *Analyst* into Test Analyst.

I wrote earlier about why agile testers should be involved from the start. It's obviously very important in agile development, and has a number of very good benefits. With User Stories, my teams have generally gone a step further.

A Business Analyst, Product Manager, Product Owner and/or the Team should identify the relevant User Stories for the Product Backlog. From this feature list, for the selected items for the next Sprint, requirements need to be clarified and expanded on.

The requirements for each User Story should be discussed and clarified as a team. But, in my view, the Test Analyst is an ideal person to lead this discussion and write up the User Stories.

Test Analysts tend to be very analytical in their nature. They tend to be good communicators. And, as we all know, they can think of scenarios that business people and developers never even dream of!

More so, when it comes to writing test confirmations for the User Story, they are obviously the ideal person to do this. Writing these test cases up-front, when the feature is being defined, helps to improve quality from the outset, as developers are more likely to write their code to pass the tests (because they know what they are).

But also, it makes perfect sense to me, for the person that's going to test a User Story, to be the person that defined it.

For this reason, agile testers can also make excellent agile analysts.

Agile Project Management

Is The Need For Projects Dead?

On BAU (Business As Usual) development, an agile approach makes a lot of sense.

Moving through iterations, working on features from the Product Backlog, collaborating with stakeholders about the requirements for each feature, delivering working software incrementally.

But what about Projects? In an agile environment, do we still need Projects? Or is everything literally broken down into small incremental pieces. And Projects, as we knew them, cease to exist? Imagine life without Projects... Bliss!

Or would teams just slip into a treadmill of ongoing Sprints and lack any real purpose?

One thing Projects definitely do provide, usually in abundance, is focus. And a real sense of pressure to deliver. With that pressure, often comes intellectual challenge, motivation, team spirit, and a bunch of other positive things too.

Unfortunately, with that pressure, projects also often come with a lot of hassle, over-spending, late delivery, features that don't meet expectations, and a lot of disappointment. But the reality is, projects are still necessary in an agile environment.

If for no other reason, they are necessary because the people funding the project (whether that's external customers or internal sponsors) expect to know what the outcome will be, if they invest their hard-earned money in your project.

What, exactly, will I get? Exactly how long will it take? What exactly will it cost? How can you assure me the project will be a success?

Obviously in traditional software development projects, people have known these details precisely, because they've specified everything up-front and planned everything in detail :)

And of course things are always then delivered to those expectations, right?

Of course not.

Of course we all know it's a false sense of security, and in reality there is little that will really assure the people funding the project that they will actually get everything they wished for, on time and in budget. According to independent research, over 70% of projects fail to meet expectations.

Fact.

But still, Board members and customers continue to expect the impossible, or at least the improbable. Expecting development teams to predict, up-front, the outcome of their project in terms of cost, time and quality/scope/features. Fixing all three dimensions.

Unfortunately, however, this is the culture in which most companies operate. It's what they are used to.

Until the 2nd or 3rd generation of agile teams is coming through, and the 1st generation of agilists are in senior positions of influence with customers or the Board, this false expectation will continue to exist.

So Projects are necessary. A necessary evil, maybe? But necessary.

Is Agile Right For Your Project?

Some argue that an agile development approach is right for any project. Others argue that agile is a hoax!

Of course the reality is somewhere in between.

I'm sure you can apply agile principles, or a more traditional approach, to any project. The best way to approach anything is often the way you know.

Although I'm sure that some projects definitely suit agile more than others.

Personally I think agile suits more projects than not - due to human nature and the evolutionary nature of software development.

But how do you know whether you should use agile for your project? Or whether or not your typical projects suit agile? How do you know if agile is right for you?

DSDM (Dynamic Systems Development Method) is one of the earliest development methodologies based on agile philosophies. The DSDM methodology includes a project suitability filter.

This filter is a simple questionnaire that attempts to highlight the key characteristics of a project that is well suited to DSDM, or more generally to an agile approach. Here are questions:

- Does the sponsor/senior management understand and accept the iterative philosophy?
- Is there senior user commitment to provide active user (or user representative) involvement?
- Can the organisation accommodate the frequent delivery of increments?
- Will it be possible for the developers to have access to users (user representatives) throughout the project?

- Will the development team remain the same throughout the project?
- Will the development team have the appropriate skills?
- Is there a supportive commercial relationship?
- Will the project use technologies suitable for prototyping?
- Is there a highly demonstrable user interface?
- Is there clear ownership?
- Will the development be computationally non-complex? (agile can be used on complex projects but complex computation lends itself less well to frequent change, prototyping and visibility)
- Can the solution be delivered in small increments?
- Does the development have a fixed timescale?
- Can the requirements be prioritised (can't all be must-haves)
- Will users be able to define requirements interactively?

Of course some of these questions are important in a non-agile approach too. But these questions are even more important for agile projects.

If you're thinking of using an agile approach, answering yes to most of the above questions is good!

If you have a few No's, this doesn't mean agile is inappropriate, although you should consider how you might mitigate these risks.

If you have lots of no's, you should think seriously about whether your project or environment is really suitable, or ask yourself honestly, is your organisation really ready for agile?

Agile Project Management Questions Answered

I was asked to answer 5 questions about agile project management for a feature on PM Boulevard. I thought you might appreciate seeing them here too...

1. How has the Agile practice evolved over the last two years?

I don't personally think that agile practices have particularly changed in the last two years, however there is clearly a stronger emphasis on some elements more than others now.

Scrum certainly seems to have crossed into the mainstream. Until a couple of years ago, Scrum still felt quite new and innovative in the UK. I work in the web development sector and now every company I meet seems to be doing Scrum.

Another change is the interest in agile from the project management community. This seems significant as people start to think more about how best to apply agile on larger projects. Looking at Google Trends, which shows search volumes over time, shows that search demand for 'agile project management' started relatively late in terms of agile adoption, and interest is still growing strongly now.

The other thing that seems to be a clear trend is a much stronger emphasis on Lean software development from the agile community. It seems to have really gathered pace in the last couple of years or so.

2. What would you tell someone who thinks Agile is just another fad?

I don't think agile can be called a fad now! Admittedly it may not be for everyone, but it's certainly not a small minority any more. Again using Google Trends to gauge search demand and therefore people's interest in a topic, 'agile software development' has been in high demand on Google as far back as 2005 (although it's obviously been around a lot longer than that), and has remained high ever since.

I don't think something can be called a fad when the buzz has been going for several years already and is continuing to grow strongly.

For anyone that hates the idea of agile and is secretly hoping it might just go away, you'd better get used to it because I think it's here to stay!

3. What are some tools that you use?

I know this might sound like it isn't much help to others, but we don't actually use any project management tools or any specific agile tools.

Those who read my blog will know I'm a big fan of Excel and the whiteboard, although clearly agile project management tools would be a useful addition in some circumstances, particularly where teams or stakeholders are distributed across multiple locations or projects are particularly large.

In my experience, I've had several development teams practicing agile web development using Scrum, and they have been able to operate Scrum on a team-by-team basis without the need for any specialist tools to help manage.

Instead we have placed a much stronger emphasis on face-to-face communication and collaboration, using Excel to manage product backlogs, user stories to convey requirements, and whiteboards to provide visibility and tracking.

4. Do you think that Agile and the PMBOK can coexist?

I definitely think agile and PMBOK can coexist, although some elements of PMBOK would be irrelevant to apply on an agile project. However there are plenty of elements of PMBOK that are not addressed at all within agile methodologies, for instance project initiation, cost management, risk management and various other aspects too.

I think the problem here is that a project manager must know PMBOK-style project management methods like PRINCE2 and agile methods such as Scrum very well to be able to choose the right techniques for the right situation. This obviously demands a lot of skill and experience from the project manager and is potentially very difficult for anyone new to either method.

This is where experienced project managers that have successfully transitioned to agile have a really strong advantage over others who have only really managed projects with one approach or the other. It gives them the ability to blend the methods based on the unique characteristics of their particular situation, which along with leadership skills might be the thing that differentiates a good project manager from a great one.

5. Can you recommend a book, blog, podcast, Web site, or other information source to our readers that you find interesting or intriguing right now?

First and foremost, I would obviously recommend you read each and every page of my blog! :) (www.allaboutagile.com). As if that's not enough, I can also recommend various others, which you'll find in my blogroll in the sidebar. My personal favourites at the moment are Leading Agile by Mike Cottmeyer, Succeeding with Agile by Mike Cohn, and Agile Techniques on InfoQ.

In terms of books, Agile Project Management with Scrum by Ken Schwaber and Agile Estimating and Planning by Mike Cohn are particularly recommended. For larger projects, the best book I've read on how to scale agile is Agile Software Requirements by Dean Leffingwell.

Agile Project Management Is Not Enough!

For agile project management, agile methodologies such as Scrum and Extreme Programming alone are not enough.

Extreme Programming (XP) is excellent for agile engineering practices that improve product quality, and User Stories from XP are an excellent way to simplify the understanding and management of requirements on a piecemeal basis.

Scrum is excellent for managing a project team's workload and delivering products incrementally through iterative development.

If you're not familiar with it, take a look at the Project Management Body Of Knowledge (PMBOK). This body of knowledge is a globally recognised standard and was put together by the PMI (Project Management Institute). It encapsulates common practices for project management irrespective of specific methodology.

PMBOK embodies all that we refer to as 'traditional' project management and is a very useful resource. No doubt it includes traditional project management practices that are not at all appropriate if you're doing agile. But it also includes key aspects of a project that need managing which are simply not addressed by Scrum or Extreme Programming. For instance:

- Project Initiation
- Cost Management
- Human Resources Management (hate that term, but important nevertheless!)
- Communications Management
- Risk Management
- Procurement Management
- Stakeholder Management
- Organisational factors

Sure, in agile we don't want to see a big specification up-front. We don't want to see every task mapped out on a huge Gantt chart. We don't want to see change control as the process for scope management. But we do need the above list of things managed in many agile projects.

So how is this overcome in practice?

In my experience, it is overcome by having a 'traditional' Project Manager, who understands project management (such as PMBOK, or the PRINCE2 project management methodology that has become the standard in the UK), who can apply the relevant aspects of the traditional PM approach with the agile practices of Scrum and Extreme Programming. Effectively augmenting agile with traditional project management methods where appropriate.

Wow! In my view that requires a lot of skill, knowledge, experience and expertise. To understand Scrum, Extreme Programming and PMBOK, and somehow to blend it all together to create a method that encompasses agile management, agile engineering and project management. All the time still retaining the agile mindset and satisfying stakeholders that are used to a more traditional project approach. And without a clear industry reference point to help convey the blended process to all stakeholders and members of the project team.

Is it my imagination, or are we missing something important in the agile community?

Is there anything similar to "PMBOK" for agile? Is there something that blends PMBOK with Scrum and XP, in order to create a comprehensive methodology for managing agile projects. Something described in a way that is easily accessible to all roles in a project, not just those that are experts in the subject?

If there is, I'd really like to hear about it...

PMBOK and Agile

When I was a project manager using more traditional project management methods, I found the PMBOK (Project Management Body Of Knowledge) really useful. Unfortunately the PMI (Project Management Institute) charge for it now, but it was useful to me at that time, pulling together all of the most common project management practices in one place.

The PMBOK is focused on project management generally rather than any specific methodology or methods particularly geared up for software development projects. Therefore it majors on more traditional project management techniques. It does acknowledge agile methods - although I believe not by name - by describing iterative development as a valid approach to the project lifecycle.

It's probably about time the PMI included a whole section on agile project management. Maybe even to talk about agile techniques in each section of the PMBOK, for instance it would be great if their estimating section covered the practice of estimating in points, tracking velocity in fixed iterations, and using that to plan future iterations.

Back in 2007, Michele Sliger wrote a set of slides that map the traditional methods in PMBOK to common agile practices. Although it's a few years old already, I personally think it's a superb piece of work and I think would help a lot of people understand the relationship between agile project management methods and more traditional project management methods.

Extending PMBOK

I have long held the belief that agile is only a part and a subset of the wider topic of project management. As I have mentioned, I feel there are various aspects of project management that aren't particularly covered by any of the most popular agile methods, or at least not by Scrum and XP (Extreme Programming).

Therefore I have always been keen to highlight the importance of project management beyond what is provided for by agile methods, and equally keen to help project managers understand where agile methods fit in to what they already know.

In the PMI's PMBOK (Project Management Body of Knowledge), agile is not specifically mentioned, however PMBOK tends to describe what a project manager should be managing, and not much about how to manage it. Arguably, agile methods tend to focus a little more on how.

Although agile and traditional project management methods place a completely different emphasis on different parts of the project lifecycle (e.g. waterfall puts a heavy emphasis on the planning phase, whereas agile does not), it is somewhat possible to augment PMBOK with agile methods, as they are partly complementary.

I hope that one day this will actually happen as an official and global standard, but in the meantime I thought I'd have a go at expanding on PMBOK (and in the same style of PMBOK), to give my view about where agile fits in with the wider discipline of project management as a whole.

PMBOK highlights 5 phases that are typical in many projects:
- Initiating
- Planning
- Executing
- Monitoring and Controlling
- Closing

I think the same phases can be and usually are applied to agile projects, but as I mentioned earlier, the emphasis and detail within the phases would change accordingly, and some of the language would also change too.

Because of the iterative nature of agile methods, all of these phases take place initially only at a very high level, and then again in more detail within each iteration or 'Sprint' (Sprint is the name given to an iteration in the Scrum agile methodology).

In PMBOK, under the Executing phase of a project, there is one particular process labelled 3.5.1 'Direct and Manage Project Execution'. PMBOK says this is the process of performing the work defined in the plan, but leaves more or less everything else to the project manager's imagination.

Of course there are sections in PMBOK about managing scope, managing resources, managing finances, managing the schedule, etc, but PMBOK tends to cover what should be done and doesn't usually explain how.

So the first extension to PMBOK that I would write for agile project management would be to drill down on 3.5.1 'Direct and Manage Project Execution' to cover managing iterations within an agile project.

I have done that below, in the same style and using similar language to PMBOK, and also retaining the PMBOK numbering system. Here it is...

3.5.1 Direct and Manage Project Execution

Direct and Manage Project Execution is the process of delivering the features defined in the Product Backlog. In agile projects, the work is performed in short, fixed-length iterations. Each iteration has 4 key processes, reflecting 4 of the phases of a typical project:

- Plan Iteration (Sprint Planning)
- Execute Iteration (Sprint)
- Monitor & Control Iteration (Manage Sprint)
- Close Iteration (Sprint Review)

3.5.1.1 Plan Iteration (Sprint Planning)

Plan Iteration (Sprint Planning) is the process of discussing what can be delivered in the next iteration, clarifying requirements for selected 'User Stories', identifying tasks and estimating the effort, and committing to the work.

Inputs
.1 Product Backlog (Prioritised)
.2 Velocity Achieved Previously
.3 Draft User Stories
.4 Team Members' Availability

Tools & Techniques
.1 Sprint Planning Meeting
.2 Estimating in Points (Fibonacci)
.3 Planning Poker

Outputs
.1 Sprint Goals & Backlog (Selected User Stories)
.2 Task Breakdown and Estimates (optionally)
.3 Team's Commitment
.4 Cards on Whiteboard

3.5.1.2 Execute Iteration (Sprint)

Execute Iteration (Sprint) is the process of producing working software as planned for the current iteration.

Inputs
.1 Sprint Backlog (Selected User Stories)
.2 Task Breakdown & Estimates

Tools & Techniques
.1 Collaboration
.2 Test Driven Development
.3 Automated Testing
.4 Continuous Integration or Daily Build
.5 Test Early & Often
.6 Pair Programming
.7 Refactoring

Outputs
.1 Working Software for Selected User Stories
.2 Test Confirmations
.3 Automated Tests
.4 Any Related Documentation

3.5.1.3 Monitor and Control Iteration (Manage Sprint)

Monitor and Control Iteration (Manage Sprint) is the process of tracking work in progress and assisting successful delivery.

Inputs
.1 Work Completed Yesterday
.2 Work Intended Today
.3 Impediments Affecting Progress
.4 Working Software for User Stories Completed So Far

Tools & Techniques
.1 Cards on Whiteboard
.2 Daily Scrum/Standup
.3 Daily Burndown or Burnup Chart
.4 Review Product Frequently / Active User Involvement
.5 Address Impediments
.6 Definition of Done

Outputs
.1 Final Burndown or Burnup Chart
.2 Velocity Achieved

3.5.1.4   Close Iteration (Sprint Review)

Close Iteration (Sprint Review) is the process of reviewing work completed in the current iteration, reviewing progress against the overall plan, reflecting on how the iteration went, and deciding how to improve in the next iteration.

Inputs
.1 Final Burndown or Burn-up Chart
.2 Velocity Achieved
.3 Working Software for Completed User Stories
.4 Feedback from Team

Tools & Techniques
.1 Sprint Review Meeting
.2 Sprint Retrospective Meeting

Outputs
.1 Demo of Completed User Stories
.2 Updated Product Backlog
.3 Retrospective Actions
.4 Updated Velocity Graph
.5 Sprint Report

These processes are repeated for each iteration until the project's objectives are achieved, or until it is decided that the objectives are no longer worth pursuing.

No Sprint Is An Island!

One of the key agile principles is about fixing timescales and varying scope.

In DSDM (Dynamic Systems Development Methodology) these fixed periods are called timeboxes; in Scrum they are called Sprints; and in XP (Extreme Programming) they are iterations.

For Business-As-Usual (BAU) changes to existing products, one Sprint may equal a release of the product. However for projects it's more than likely multiple Sprints will be required before the features have enough value to the user to be worth releasing.

In the case of projects, it's clear there must be some kind of Release Planning sitting over the individual Sprints. This is important to estimate how many Sprints are likely to be required before the product will be ready to be released.

Having done this release planning and worked out how many Sprints should be needed, probably doing some fairly high level estimating at the outset in order to secure project funding, individual Sprints cannot be run in isolation.

The danger if they are, is that any overhang (or personally I prefer to call it hangover!) accumulates and creates a bow-wave effect towards the end of the project, and on some projects it's more like a tsunami!

Whilst the scope may be varied, and in agile development the scope should be varied, there does of course come a point when you simply can't vary scope any further without seriously undermining the basis of the original business case. And unfortunately it's at that point you're back to the good old-fashioned slippage, that is all-too-common and all-too-painful in so many software development projects using whatever methodology.

So how about BAU? Surely you can run individual Sprints in BAU, each leading to a release of the product? Yes, technically you can. But I say you shouldn't.

Just to clarify - yes, of course you can run individual Sprints each leading to a release of the product. But ideally you shouldn't run a sequence of Sprints in complete isolation, even in the BAU scenario.

The Product Owner, together with the product team and those responsible for the commercial results of the product, should ideally form an outline plan of sorts; a high level roadmap if you will. This is important as the basis for business planning, budgets, revenue forecasts, etc. And even if the planning is fairly unscientific at this level, there must be a clear business vision of the key drivers for the product over time, and this vision needs to inform the priorities of the Sprints.

Prioritisation Using MoSCoW

Several years after I first encountered it, I still find MoSCoW one of the easiest methods for prioritisation.

The MoSCoW approach to prioritisation originated from the DSDM methodology (Dynamic Software Development Method), which was possibly the first agile methodology (?) - even before we knew iterative development as 'agile'.

MoSCoW is a fairly simple way to sort features (or User Stories) into priority order - a way to help teams quickly understand the customer's view of what is essential for launch and what is not.

MoSCoW stands for:
- **Must** have (or sometimes known as Minimum Usable Subset, or Minimum Viable Product)
- **Should** have
- **Could** have
- **Won't** have (but Would like in future!)

'Must Haves' are features that must be included before the product can be launched. It is good to have clarity on this before a project begins, as this is the minimum scope for the product to be useful.

'Should Haves' are features that are not critical to launch, but are considered to be important and of a high value to the user.

'Could Haves' are features that are nice to have and could potentially be included without incurring too much effort or cost. These will be the first features to be removed from scope if the project's timescales are later at risk.

'Won't Haves' are features that have been requested but are explicitly excluded from scope for the planned duration, and may be included in a future phase of development.

It's a good idea to make sure a project has a healthy number of Should Have and Could Have requirements. This helps to provide the project with some flexibility if things start taking longer than expected, effectively providing the project with some contingency.

If a project only has 'Must Haves', the scope cannot be varied. Therefore the cost and timescales should not really be fixed without including a reasonable contingency. 'Could Haves' can be that contingency. They are effectively stretch tasks; features that will be included if possible, but the launch date will not be moved to accommodate them if there is not enough time to complete them.

How To Prioritise Quickly And Intuitively

If you're in a situation where prioritisation is straightforward and you have a single decisive product owner, you probably need to read no further.

If, however, prioritisation is difficult in your situation - maybe because you have several products or product owners with conflicting priorities, or maybe because your requirements can be complex and benefits rather intangible - this is for you. In this case, prioritisation can be difficult and priorities are not always immediately obvious.

This simple approach might help you to prioritise more quickly...

Draw a 2 x 2 grid. Use the bottom axis as 'Difficulty'. Make the vertical axis 'Importance'.

'Difficulty' should represent all the negative aspects, such as time, cost, effort, risk, complexity, etc. High difficulty to the left, low difficulty is to the right.

The 'Importance' axis should represent all the positive aspects, such as revenue, cost-savings, and (slightly counter-intuitively) the risk of not doing it. Low importance at the bottom, high at the top.

'Difficulty' could be your complexity points if your using Fibonacci estimating or something similar. But it doesn't really matter. The important thing is simply one item's difficulty and importance relative to another.

Plot each of your items on the grid, making an intuitive judgement about whether it's harder or easier, more or less important, than the other items already plotted. Make sure they're plotted roughly in the right position, relative to each other.

Get the relevant product owners to decide on the vertical position.

Get the technical team to decide on the horizontal position. This is best done in a workshop with all the relevant people together. It's also important that only those qualified to judge should influence the horizontal position!

It's a good idea to start with the things that are clearly the easiest, hardest, most and least important. Place these in the corners of the grid to provide a useful context for other, less obvious items.

Once you've got all your things on the grid, think about the four quadrants.

Things in the top right are "No-Brainers". These things are clear priorities.

Things in the bottom left are potentially for the bin, as these things are of the least value. Or at least you can stop worrying about them for now.

Things in the bottom right are quite straightforward to deliver but not the most important. Consider ways to make them more valuable, i.e. push them up on the grid. Could they be chargeable features (if appropriate)? Or if enhanced slightly would they be considered much more important? Of course you shouldn't do this artificially, as it could be counter-productive.

Typically things in the top left quadrant are more strategic developments. Although they're over to the left, if you never start them you'll certainly never deliver them. Consider ways to simplify these items. Consider breaking them up into multiple things, so bits can move to the right on the grid and the strategic changes delivered over time.

This might sound like a simplistic approach, but you might be surprised how many things you're already working on that are not in the top right of the grid. And how many things you might not be working on, that are.

How To Prioritise - Get More Bang For Your Buck!

I love the way the 2x2 grid I described in the previous pages provides a really quick and easy way to prioritise, and a way to look at priorities more visually.

Rather than just positioning the items where you think they belong on the grid, you could also consider plotting the Importance axis using points representing Business Value. Score importance 1-10, or 1-100 if you want more granularity, whatever you prefer. Or maybe even use Fibonacci numbers to score relative importance the same as you do for estimating each feature's size.

As well as giving you the grid above, you can also use these two sets of numbers to calculate a value:effort ratio for all the things in your list of priorities.

This ratio, being a number, allows you to quickly sort your priorities into an order that represents how to deliver the highest value fastest, rather than just highest value first.

Agile Project Initiation

I wrote earlier about how I think Agile Project Management alone is not enough. Project Initiation is one of the areas of agile methods that I think needs embellishment for large projects.

Over the years, I've used quite a few techniques for project initiation. But I've never really come across an agile one.

My first experience of formal project initiation was a Project Definition Report in Method1, a very traditional methodology from Anderson Consulting as they were known then; now Accenture.

Later, as a Project Manager, I used a PID (Project Initiation Document) from the PRINCE2 project management methodology, which I guess is probably the most widely used today.

In MSF (Microsoft Solutions Framework), there's the Vision & Scope document.

Truth is, they're all pretty similar really. Long documents, with lots of details about a project and how it's going to be run. Long, tedious documents.

Yet, for large projects, they are important.

As a Project Manager, I always found the thought process they made me go through was incredibly useful. I personally benefited from writing them; that's for sure. Without them, the project could be poorly thought through. And the chances of failure would certainly be higher.

So the thinking was valuable. Trouble was, no-one wanted to read those lengthy documents. All that thinking. All that writing! And no-one was really interested, truth be known. Not the Project Board. Not the project team. And certainly not the wider stakeholders.

So, if the thinking is valuable, what do agile methods have to offer instead?

Nothing.

Unless I've missed it somehow. Nothing.

So, for large projects that warrant it, how do we incorporate this valuable thinking into agile methods? And how do we do it in a way that people will actually pay any attention to? The answer is simple.

Do it in PowerPoint.

Producing this information in PowerPoint has some profound effects:

- It's easier to write. In PowerPoint, the writer is naturally more concise, because of the constraints of the format.

- It's easier to read. It's natural in PowerPoint to convey things in a more interesting and digestible form.

- And it's easier to share. Invite people to a meeting or presentation, and they'll happily sit through a PowerPoint to understand the goals of a project. The speaker - aided by the slides - brings the information alive. Ask the same people to read a 50 page project initiation document and, surprise surprise, the response is different.

Thinking a project through before kicking it off is valuable.

Being able to communicate this thinking to others is imperative. To get funding; to share the vision with the team; to inform other stakeholders about the goals of the project.

So next time you need to do a more formal project initiation, why not try it in a format that's more appropriate for the purpose?

Agile Project Elaboration: Seed Money

In traditional waterfall projects, it's quite common to have a two-stage approval process, especially when it comes to raising funds to develop a new idea.

Stage 1 approval provides sufficient funding to get a project started and complete the analysis phase. Once analysis has been completed and a detailed specification written, the project can be more accurately estimated and a further request is made for full funding of the project.

So how would you tackle an agile project with this kind of approach to the funding?

First of all, this two-stage approval process for funding a new project is still valid with an agile approach. It's simply an unavoidable reality that some work has to be done before a project can be reasonably well understood and estimated. And this work, unless there's a permanent team already in place, needs funding before an investment decision can be made.

So, in an agile project, what outputs might you produce with the initial funding? You certainly wouldn't want to complete a full analysis phase and detailed specification. But you would need something.

Here are some ideas of what you could produce with this initial seed money:

- Visuals or Wireframes
- Research (User/Customer/Market Research)
- Prototype
- Proof of Concept
- Technical Feasibility Study
- Initial Product Backlog (feature list)
- High-level Architecture

- Technology Selection
- Initial Estimates
- Team/Resource Requirements
- Forecast Release Plan/Product Roadmap
- Costs
- Business Case
- Project Initiation Presentation

Whether or not you produce all of this depends entirely on your project, of course, and whether or not you feel it is of value. In any case it should be high level, not fully comprehensive. Sufficient to shape the project and understand the requirements and solution better. Sufficient to understand how much funding should be requested to complete the project. No more.

If initial funding permits, you may also be able to establish the project team and complete a few short sprints, in order to understand the team's Velocity for planning purposes. But this would depend not only on the initial funds available, but also on the likelihood of full approval.

The Problem With Planning

I think I've been pretty successful in my career. But if I was better at planning, I wouldn't have achieved half the things I've achieved in my career! In fact, I wouldn't even have started some of them...

In reality, there are some things you can plan, and some things you can't.

The trouble is, in most organisations we've come to expect a plan. And to meet it whatever happens. And that's just not realistic.

Doing detailed planning pre-supposes you know where you want to go and aren't going to be influenced too much by what happens in the meantime - or at least not without a substantial amount of re-planning. This, at least in my experience, has a tendency to give project managers tunnel vision at times.

Now don't get me wrong - I'm not suggesting for one moment you embark on a project that doesn't have a clear and robust vision. And I'm not suggesting for a moment you embark on a project where you have no idea how to achieve it and whether it's a reasonable (although hopefully challenging) goal with the available resources. And forming that into an outline plan to provide some markers to aim for is certainly a good idea, but ideally it's a high level roadmap rather than a detailed plan.

Coming from a traditional software development environment, I realise this sounds slightly mad. And I must admit it takes a certain amount of maturity and experience to recognise that you can't really plan in detail up-front if you want to retain any flexibility, as the real requirements, risks, issues, priorities and opportunities all tend to emerge when you start to build and see the software in action.

Most organisations are not ready to accept such a radical idea - the idea of acknowledging you don't really know what you want - certainly not for sure - and you don't really know what you're going to get for your money, or when. So, as a minimum, a clear vision and outline plan are essential, but be careful to keep them to a high level.

Rather than a detailed plan, I prefer to see a strong vision, a strategy, goals, and a roadmap (high level outline plan). The tactics to achieve this, for example the precise features and all the tasks to deliver them, can vary along the way and are best not articulated up-front. This enables the team to discover the details when they are in a better position to do so, and allows them to change direction rapidly in response to changing circumstances.

This, when you think of it, is the very meaning of agile...

Agile Project Planning

Sometimes I think projects are a necessary evil. But necessary they are.

Some people really feel the need to understand precisely what the project will cost and exactly long it will take. If this is the basis for investment, of course that's a completely understandable feeling.

For years, traditional waterfall projects have been sold on the false pretense that projects are predictable. Plannable. Of course the reality is, projects are highly unpredictable, and - sadly - that's why so many projects fail to meet expectations.

So when you need to plan a project, in order to forecast the overall costs and timescales, how do you do this for an agile project?

Well, of course, agile development is no silver bullet.

If you are bad at planning, bad at identifying and sticking to at least the broad scope of the project, bad at estimating until you have all the details, bad at controlling delivery, an agile project plan is likely to be just as bad as a non-agile one!

The benefits of agile development are more to do with early realisation of business value, early visibility when things are going off track, collaboration and regular feedback to ensure quality and provide the right solution, and so on.

Yes, there are also some important benefits in the approach to estimating, but fundamentally, planning a complete project up-front and committing to costs and timescales is still, of course, a potentially potted process. A process full of pitfalls. And a process that requires great skill and experience to get anywhere close to predicting something that will resemble reality.

But, with that caveat in mind, here's how agile project planning works...

Agile project planning is generally referred to as 'Release Planning'. The concept of an agile release plan is about planning multiple Sprints that culminate in a release of the product. It is not necessarily project-oriented, however the concept for projects is of course the same.

Product Backlog

First of all, you really need to get your Product Backlog in order!

The Product Backlog is essentially a feature list. Above all, it's user-oriented and lists features in a language that business people and users understand. It's not technical. And it's not a list of tasks. Do not attempt to list all the tasks for the project and identify all the dependencies. Just list all the features the project needs to deliver.

Also include any lasting deliverables that are not necessarily part of the software. For example a User Manual, or a Technical Reference Document for any API's. However do not list the temporary deliverables that are just part of delivering a feature. For example don't list the analysis tasks or design documents for each feature. Try to keep it as a list of product features and only include deliverables that outlive the project.

What I'm about to say is an important point about any planning process, whether it's agile or not.

There are generally only two things that cause your plan to fail:
1) You under-estimate the things you've identified; and/or
2) You don't manage to identify everything.

Since you probably only estimate the items you identify, the quality of your Product Backlog is a critical success factor for your project.

Business Analysis

So surely I have to do a complete analysis up-front to make sure I've identified everything, right?

Yes and no.

If you're going to plan a complete project, even if it's an agile project, you do need to do enough analysis to identify all the features you think you need to deliver.

However, unlike in a traditional analysis with a specification, you really do not need to identify all the details about how each feature will work. Just enough analysis to list all the features, with a degree of confidence that the broad scope of the system is covered. The details can be left until later, and be dealt with just in time for the feature to be developed.

So it's very important that the Product Backlog is at an appropriate level of detail. This, in itself, is a mysterious art. If the items are too detailed, and you estimate only what you've identified, there is a high chance you'll miss some things out. But if the items are not detailed enough, there's a high chance your estimates will be wrong.

Because agile estimating is based on broad, relative size of each feature, you do not have to break down the features too small at this early stage when trying to estimate the overall project.

For example, it's probably sufficient to know that users will need to be able to register and log in. It's probably not necessary to itemise what details they will need to enter to register, and how the system will authenticate the login. Unlike traditional projects, you certainly don't need to worry about how long will the fields be and what validation will be needed, and minor details like that. The details can be sorted out later.

When you are reasonably confident you have a comprehensive Product Backlog that broadly covers the scope of the project, listing all the features that need to be delivered by the project - not too detailed but detailed enough to compare the relative size of each feature - you are ready to do your estimates.

Estimating

First of all, do your estimates as a team. 'Planning poker' is a method where each team member writes their estimate on a card and all team members reveal their estimate at the same time. This is quite fun to do and is a great way to get everyone's estimate before they are influenced by others. Wild discrepancies in people's estimates are a great discussion point, a way to identify differences in understanding early on, and a way to understand different people's perspectives about the implementation.

Secondly, estimate your features in points. Many agile teams use the Fibonacci numbering system to do this. The points represent the relative size of each feature. For example, a feature with a 2 is roughly twice the size of a 1, which is very simple. A feature with a 5 is a bit more than twice the size of a 2, and a 21 is much more difficult.

Basically it's the relatively of this estimating approach that is important, not the number itself.

The philosophy is that people can't really tell you accurately how many days or hours it will take to implement something they know little about, but they can tell you generally whether they expect it, on average, to be easier or harder than something else.

When the whole Product Backlog has been estimated, you now know the 'size' of your project, but it's in abstract points rather than in real units of time. How do you convert this into a cost and timescale?

Planning

If you are going to utilise an existing team that are already doing agile, and you know their average Velocity per Sprint, it's easy. Just calculate how many Sprints it would take to burn-down the number of points on your project's product backlog.

If, however, you're establishing a new team, that has not done agile before, you have no idea what their Velocity might be and this is another potted part of the planning process. Basically you need to make an assumption about the team size and its Velocity. In this case, this how I would do it...

Get more than 1 developer, of varying skill and experience, to look at a small section of the Product Backlog. Ask them how much they think they could complete in a single Sprint. Remember to explain what you mean by complete, i.e. done means DONE!, so you know everyone is working to the same basic assumptions.

Compare the number of points each developer has effectively said they can complete in a Sprint and decide what you consider to be a reasonable average based on what you've heard. Using that average number of points, assume that's your Velocity (per person) and calculate the number of Sprints you would need to complete the entire Product Backlog. This calculation will give you your approximate project duration based on 1 developer.

Summary

Now you can make an assumption about the size of your team, based on the available people, the target timescales or the amount of funding you could potentially raise, and cost it up accordingly.

As with all projects, it would be wise to add a contingency. As I mentioned earlier, it's often the features you didn't list that cause a plan to fail. The contingency should reflect your level of confidence in the quality of the Product Backlog. If you think it is thorough, and the project is unlikely to be prone to lots of change, maybe you should add about 10-20% to your project. Otherwise it might be wise to add more.

Remember, though - although agile estimating and planning does have some distinct advantages, it is not a silver bullet. The care and attention you put into this process, along with the skill and experience of your team, in the end will really determine how likely your plan is to succeed.

Track Your Agile Projects With A Project Burndown Chart

Agile project management often needs more than the practices provided as standard by agile methods. Tracking project status is one area where I think that's true.

Scrum includes the concept of a Sprint Burndown Chart. It's a simple yet very powerful concept. Here's a reminder of how it works...

At the start of each Sprint, the team has estimated the work they plan to complete in the Sprint, either in days, hours or in points. Let's assume points. The burndown chart has the days of the Sprint across the bottom axis. On the first day of the Sprint, the number plotted on the chart is the total planned points for the Sprint.

Each day, this total is reduced for any items that are completed, so the total gradually reduces, hopefully until it reaches zero at the end of the Sprint.

You can also draw a target line from the top left of the chart to the bottom right, assuming that every day the same number of points are 'burnt down'.

If your actual line is below the target, you're on track. If it's above, you're falling behind.

And that's the beauty of the burndown chart. You can see very clearly - literally at a glance - how the team is doing against their Sprint plan for the current iteration.

Extreme Programming, by the way, has the same concept, but in XP you burn up rather than down.

So what's a Project Burndown Chart?

It's an adaptation of the Sprint burndown chart, designed to give you the same sort of clarity, but at a project level, rather than for an individual Sprint.

Use a similar format to the daily Sprint burndown chart, but instead of days along the bottom, put Sprints. At the start of the chart, plot the total size of the Product Backlog for the entire project.

For your target line, reduce the number for each Sprint by your target or forecast Velocity (the number of points you expect to burn down in each Sprint).

As you complete each Sprint, reduce your actual number by your Velocity and the actual line will start to come down, hopefully as fast as your target line!

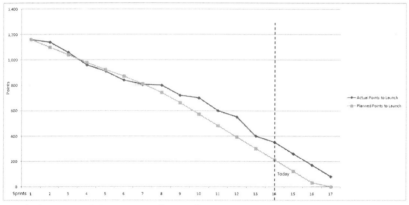

And that's it! It's as simple as that.

When you have a project that spans multiple Sprints, it can be hard to keep track of where you really are. With a Project Burndown Chart, it's easy. And best of all, it hardly takes any time at all to produce and doesn't require you to do any additional planning.

I've never seen a Gantt chart and traditional status report provide the same incredible clarity that a Project Burndown Chart does. It's brilliantly simple, and it's quantitative, rather than a matter of opinion.

If you have multiple projects on the go, across several teams, there is no quicker way to know which projects are on track and which are struggling, and with a fraction of the paperwork and effort of a traditional PMO (Project Management Office).

Track Scope And Progress With A Burn-Up Chart

As I mentioned before, Extreme Programming has a Burn-Up Chart rather than the Burndown Chart in Scrum. It's the same concept, but it goes up rather than down.

Why does that matter?

Well it took me a while to realise why Burn-Up Charts can be better for the team. This is why...

With a Burndown Chart, there are two factors affecting the rate at which the line comes down. One is the number of points that a team delivers. The other is the scope. Because the line is tracking the total number of points remaining, increases in scope have the effect of slowing down the burndown. Although this can be annotated, this can have two negative effects:

1. It can reflect badly on the team, making it appear that they are delivering less than they actually are - especially if it flatlines due to points being added to the backlog.

2. It also does not highlight scope changes, which is an important thing to control in its own right.

A Burn-Up Chart, on the other hand alleviates this, because two lines are plotted on the graph. One is the number of points delivered by the team, so the line goes up as more and more work is completed. The other line is for scope - a separate line on the graph representing the total number of points on the Product Backlog.

By tracking these two things separately, you get clear visibility of the scope line and when it moves. If it continues to move up, as new things are added to the scope of the project, it is highlighted clearly and shows that the team is actually up against a moving target.

The other line, representing the team's progress, continues to move up as and when things are delivered, showing the true progress of the team, independently of changes in scope.

The project will have delivered all its scope when the team's progress line reaches the scope line.

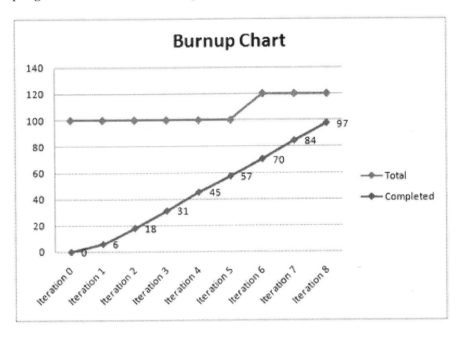

It's just as simple to produce as a Project Burndown Chart. Just as clear to read. And with a little more insight into whether it's the team's progress that is causing things to look tricky, or moving scope.

Large Agile Projects Require Some New Skills

A common question is how to run large agile projects? Answer: You don't! You break them into multiple small projects. But that puts greater emphasis on two disciplines that many organisations simply don't have...

Agile architecture, and Agile programme management.

Admittedly, the discipline of Programme Management is similar to Project Management. Maybe more experienced Project Managers can run programmes. But there is a subtle difference and it requires a different approach.

And the discipline of Programme Architecture is different to Solution Design. Maybe I've been unlucky, but in my experience this is a scarce skill.

Programme Architects need the ability to have a deeply technical background, yet also be able to see the bigger picture. The ability to bridge the gap between business vision and technology solution. The ability to distill complex problems into clear solutions, with minimised and clear dependencies. The ability to break a solution into loosely coupled, independent elements that can be developed separately by autonomous agile teams.

For me, having these skills is a critical success factor for major projects - especially with an agile development approach, because of the incremental nature of it. Without these skills, you run the very real risk of failure.

Keeping Sight of the Bigger Picture

With an agile development approach, there is no big spec and no big design up-front. Scope is variable. Requirements emerge and evolve. Features can be added, changed and removed throughout the project lifecycle.

So, with this moving target, how do you keep sight of the bigger picture?

Although agile development is all about breaking things down - breaking things down into micro pieces and delivering on a piecemeal basis - it is also very important to have some overall guiding context.

From my perspective, this context comes in 3 major forms:
* Business Context
* Project Context
* Solution Context

Business Context
What is the business vision? What are the challenges and opportunities from a business point of view? What are the business goals - short, medium and longer term? Who are the customers? Why do they buy, and what do they use the solution for? What do they like and dislike about the product? Who is the competition and what are their solutions like?
Without this over-arching contextual information, any product development team is working with a major disadvantage.

In my experience, development people can be quite innovative. With this information - if development teams have a real insight into the business context - people on the development team can be proactive. Without necessarily being asked to work on a problem, or without being asked to come up with an idea, solutions to problems and new innovations will come to mind.

Project Context

If the development team is working on a project, many of the things defined in a more traditional project initiation phase are just as important in an agile development environment.

What is the specific problem or opportunity that the project is seeking to address? What is the vision? What are the objectives? What is the scope (broadly speaking)? What is the likely cost and timeframe? What are the benefits and how will they be realised? Who will work on the project and what is the project structure?

The answers to these questions (and more, of course) give people important guidance. And that guidance is more important than ever in an agile development approach, because of the freedom to change things along the way.

With this guidance, the project team has some parameters to work within, and a clear understanding of the expected outcomes.

Solution Context

I'm a big fan of User Stories. I've written quite a lot on my blog about them, and how to write good User Stories. I love the fact they are so small. So self contained. So manageable. It really does keep things simple. But what should you do before you get down to the detail of individual User Stories?

It is important to look at individual User Stories in context of the overall solution. So what artifacts help us to do this? There may be others, but here are some things I certainly like to see before getting down to User Stories on a Sprint-by-Sprint basis:

- High-level Roadmap - broad timeline across the top, perhaps in months or quarters; highlighting key product features or milestones. Unlike a plan, a Roadmap is indicative and evolves as things change. This provides the team with some structure around Sprint Planning, with the Roadmap helping to inform the priorities of each Sprint and set Sprint Goals.

- High-level Visuals - this could be wireframes for key screens, creative visuals of a web site, a conceptual story board for the UI (User Interface), etc. Whatever form it takes, it's a high level outline of how the solution will hang together from a user's perspective. The visuals don't need to cover every single screen. They don't need to show every feature. And the solution may not look exactly like the visuals when it's finished. In fact it almost certainly won't. But it's a guide to what's intended at the outset, and should cover the main scenarios for an everyday user.

- High-level Solution Architecture - this doesn't need to be a detailed design, but you do need some architectural guidance in order to understand key technologies, product structure and how the overall solution hangs together from a technical perspective. In my view, this can be an evolving picture, the kind of thing that is sketched on a whiteboard at the start of the project, with more details being filled in as the project progresses and as technical decisions are taken.

So, in summary, an agile development team might break things into small pieces and deliver incrementally, but this makes it even more important to have the overall context always in mind. My advice would be to keep key guidance artifacts (such as project objectives, product roadmap, solution architecture) high level, lightweight and visual, and stick them on the wall along with the team's User Stories and daily tasks.

How Can I Be Sure My Agile Project Will Deliver On Time?

In agile development the timescale is fixed. So one thing you can be absolutely sure about, is that it'll deliver on time!

The question in agile development is the other way up - how can I be sure enough features will be delivered to achieve the objectives and realise the benefits?

And the truth is, that's still a really tough question.

Unfortunately, no methodology - agile or otherwise - can completely mitigate the risks of software development, because it's inherently a potent cocktail of unpredictability (people, software, estimates, change).

However agile development does provide clear, measurable, visible progress on a frequent basis, so it goes a long way in mitigating risks and identifying issues early, while there's still time to react.

Most IT Projects Fail. Will Yours?

Studies on project failure are easy to find and make depressing reading. Gartner studies suggest that 75% of all US IT projects are considered to be failures by those responsible for initiating them.

But what do they mean by failure?

They mean the solutions fundamentally did not do what was agreed. Or they missed deadlines. And/or came in over budget. Indeed half of the projects exceeded budget by over 200%!

A Standish Group study, again in the US IT industry, found that 31% of projects were cancelled outright and that the performance of 53% of the all projects was so worrying that they were challenged.

Some questions that need to be answered in assessing whether a project is fundamentally a success or failure?

- Has the project satisfied the business requirements of the primary stakeholders?

- Were the deliverables produced on time and within budget (or as amended by agreed change control)?

- Do the business owners perceive the project to be successful?

- Has the project delivered the business value promised in the original case for doing it?

I've scanned the Internet and read all sorts of articles and research on project failure, and consolidated them into a long list of reasons why IT projects most commonly fail. I've managed to eliminate all the duplicate reasons and boil it all down to these common areas, although it's still quite a long list, unfortunately for IT and project managers!

Project Initiation & Planning Issues
- Unclear or unconvincing business case
- Insufficient or non-existent approval process
- Poor definition of project scope and objectives
- Insufficient time or money given to project
- Lack of business ownership and accountability
- Insufficient and/or over-optimistic planning
- Poor estimating
- Long or unrealistic timescales; forcing project end dates despite best estimates
- Lack of thoroughness and diligence in project startup phases

Technical & Requirements Issues
- Lack of user involvement (resulting in expectation issues)
- Product owner unclear or consistently not available
- Scope creep; lack of adequate change control
- Incomplete or changing requirements
- Wrong or inappropriate technology choices
- Unfamiliar/changing technologies; lack of required skills
- Integration problems during implementation
- Poor or insufficient testing before go-live
- Lack of QA for key deliverables
- Long and unpredictable bug fixing phase at end of project

Stakeholder Management & Team Issues
- Insufficient attention to stakeholders and their needs; failure to manage expectations
- Lack of senior management/executive support; project sponsors not 100% committed to the objectives; lack understanding of the project and not actively involved
- Inadequate visibility of project status
- Denial adopted in preference to hard truths
- People not dedicated to project; trying to balance too many different priorities
- Project team members lack experience and do not have the required skills
- Team lacks authority or decision making ability
- Poor collaboration, communication and teamwork

232

Project Management Issues
- No project management best practices
- Weak ongoing management; inadequately trained or inexperienced project managers
- Inadequate tracking and reporting; not reviewing progress regularly or diligently enough
- Ineffective time and cost management
- Lack of leadership and/or communication skills

I'm sure we've all seen projects with all or some of these issues. You know, those projects other people run! :)

In reality, probably ALL projects have many of these issues. But somewhere there is a threshold. An undefined point where the issues are material to a project's chance of success, or its likelihood to fail. If only we knew where that point was!

A few things struck me when compiling this list:

Not one article or piece of research I read (and I read quite a few!) mentioned risk management. Not one. Lack of proactive risk management. Inability to identify or mitigate risks. Lack of focus on risks. Not one article or piece of research that I found. So that got me thinking. If we don't seem to acknowledge risk management, and we certainly don't seem to see it as a cause of failure, are we to believe that we as an IT industry have got risk management cracked? And if so, why do so many of our projects fail?

Secondly I was thinking about how agile principles help to mitigate these risks? I have a strong view that agile methods help with some of these areas a lot, although I'm not sure all. And it also got me thinking that I don't recall reading about any formal mechanism or process for risk management within agile methods - unless I've missed or forgotten it. There's quite a bit of risk management inherently built into agile principles and practices, but there doesn't seem to be any explicit risk management discipline.

233

Thirdly, I started thinking about risk management in more formal project management methodologies such as PRINCE2. Risk management is certainly a key discipline there. But one of the key things I was taught as a PRINCE2-based Project Manager (once upon a time I was one), was to only highlight risks unique to the project, because there's no need to highlight the usual risks. We all know software development projects might run late, for instance. So we don't need to articulate it on a formal project proposal, or in the risk log, etc. But if we don't articulate and mitigate the usual risks, aren't we ignoring the risks most likely to cause our project to fail?

Why Most IT Projects Fail - How Agile Principles Help

Here I take a quick look at the common reasons for project failure, and how I think agile software development methods and agile principles mitigate these risks and issues.

I have a strong view that agile methods help significantly with a lot of these areas of project risk, although I'm sure not all. This is an enormous subject, so I can't really do it justice and keep this to a reasonable length. So you'll just have to take or leave my comments on face value.

Here's how I think agile principles help, in my experience:

Project Initiation & Planning Issues

Unclear or unconvincing business case
Agile principles don't help directly with the business case - in fact it can be hard to make a business case for agile projects due to their agile (i.e. unpredictable) nature. However the principles of incremental delivery and frequent delivery of products can help to get an initial solution out, test the proposition with the market and get real customer feedback to inform the priorities for further development.

Insufficient or non-existent approval process
Agile business cases and new business propositions benefit from the same diligence and challenge before investing large amounts of money, just as in any other approach to development.

Poor definition of project scope and objectives
Agile projects also benefit from clear definition of scope and objectives, even though details are allowed to emerge throughout the development.

Insufficient time or money given to project
If only agile could solve this!

Lack of business ownership and accountability
Active user involvement, or involvement from a key user representative in the business, creates an environment that fosters close collaboration and cooperation.

Insufficient and/or over-optimistic planning
This is an interesting one. I (like many agile enthusiasts) believe that it's practically impossible to plan every detail of many software development projects up front, hence expectations are better managed by active involvement in the project, frequent delivery of product on an incremental basis.

Poor estimating
Agile methods provide some important principles to help with accuracy of estimating: estimating should be done by the whole team as a collaborative process; tasks should be broken down into micro pieces (ideally less than 1 day) so progress is measurable on a daily basis; 'velocity' is calculated on the number of estimated hours delivered only when a feature is 100% complete, providing a gauge for how much development can be safely included in future iterations. In non agile methods, this approach can also be adopted and is known as 'earned value analysis'. So even if you're terrible at estimating, this approach can be self correcting as long as you're consistently terrible!

Long or unrealistic timescales; forcing project end dates despite best estimates
Agile projects encourage short and regular iterations, developing the software and delivering working product in small bite-sized pieces.

Lack of thoroughness and diligence in project startup
Rather than diligent and thorough planning, agile principles propose to deliver small increments of working product and get continuous feedback from active user involvement throughout the development cycle.

Technical & Requirements Issues

Lack of user involvement (resulting in expectation issues)
Active user involvement and continuous feedback is one of the most important principles of an agile approach.

Product owner unclear or consistently not available
One of the reasons product owners are unclear in traditional projects is because they are asked for far more detail than they can handle, too early in a project and when they cannot visualise the solution. Instead, agile requirements are kept lightweight and visual, and delivered just in time for a feature to be developed. Availability must be forthcoming for agile principles to work, as it's essential for constant collaboration.

Scope creep; lack of adequate change control
Agile projects may stick to the broad scope of the project, but requirements are allowed to emerge and evolve. However the project must include non-essential requirements at the outset, in order for emerging requirements to be traded with original scope.

Poor or no requirements definition; incomplete or changing requirements
Agile projects expect requirements to be incomplete and changing. That's the nature of software. Instead of resisting this, agile projects provide for it by allowing requirements are allowed to emerge and evolve. Requirements being produced on a feature-by-feature basis, just in time to be developed, helps with definition because it breaks this intensive task into small pieces instead of being a mammoth effort up front.

Wrong or inappropriate technology choices
Agile projects can surface inappropriate technology choices early, as they encourage frequent delivery of product on an incremental basis. Testing is integrated throughout the development cycle, testing each feature as it's developed. Doing so can help to ensure inappropriate technology choices are identified early, before too much of the software has been developed.

Unfamiliar or changing technologies; lack of required skills
Agile methods don't help directly with this issue, although can help
to surface such issues early, and make them visible.

Integration problems during implementation
Agile projects are delivered in short iterations, with testing
integrated throughout the development. This requires continuous
integration of the code and frequent builds, removing the need for a
lengthy or problematic integration phase at the end of the project.

Poor or insufficient testing before go-live
Testing is integrated throughout the development.

Lack of QA for key deliverables
Working software is the key measure of progress, as the software is
developed and delivered in regular iterations. This helps to ensure
that the adequacy of any other deliverables is highlighted early and
made visible.

Long and unpredictable bug fixing phase at end of project
Testing is integrated throughout the development.

Stakeholder Management & Team Issues

**Insufficient attention to stakeholders and their needs; failure to
manage expectations**
Active user involvement ensures two way feedback throughout the
development.

**Lack of senior management/executive support; project sponsors
not 100% committed to the objectives; lack understanding of the
project and not actively involved**
All projects need this, agile or otherwise.

Inadequate visibility of project status
Agile projects provide clear visibility of measurable progress on a
daily basis.

Denial adopted in preference to hard truths
Humans, eh? Who needs 'em!

People not dedicated to project; too many different priorities
I don't think this ideal is specific only to agile methods, but agile principles propose small, multi-disciplined teams dedicated to the development of the product.

Project team members lack experience and do not have the required skills
Agile principles may help to surface such issues early, as they may well be evident in early iterations of the software. Frequent delivery of iterations and continuous testing can help to mitigate this risk when it might otherwise go unnoticed until later in the project.

Team lacks authority or decision making ability
Agile teams must be empowered.

Poor collaboration, communication and teamwork
Close collaboration between all stakeholders is essential.

Project Management Issues

No project management best practices
Can be an issue when applying agile methods, unless using an agile management practice such as Scrum.

Weak ongoing management; inadequately trained or inexperienced project managers
Agile methods and principles are just management tools. A fool with a tool is still a fool!

Inadequate tracking and reporting; not reviewing progress regularly or diligently enough
Agile practices have daily status reporting built into the process, providing clear visibility and measurable progress on a very regular basis.

Ineffective time and cost management
Daily visibility of measurable progress.

Lack of leadership and/or communication skills
Sadly, adopting agile principles doesn't make inspirational leaders.
However agile principles do encourage a particular form of servant
leadership, empowering the team to take responsibility and make
timely decisions.

Of course most of the things I've cited as agile mitigations can be
applied in any project methodology, including waterfall. It's just that
they are more the norm and explicitly emphasised in agile principles
and practices, which is something I really like.

Most of all, agile principles help enormously with visibility,
collaboration and engagement. This can transform the levels of trust
and teamwork between the product team and its key stakeholders.
The consequence of this is enhanced satisfaction, due to a much
greater understanding of the commitment and expertise of the team,
and the issues and risks they face. If failure, by definition, is a
problem of not meeting expectations, you're half way there when
you adopt an agile approach.

However, all this, in the end, ultimately still relies heavily on the
skills of the team. Just because agile methods state these principles
and have some inherent risk management built within the process, it
doesn't mean the team necessarily has all the skills and experience it
needs to execute the principles consistently.

Agile Risk Management

A risk is an uncertain event that will impact your chosen path should it be realised. Risks are events that are not currently affecting you - they haven't happened yet. Once a risk is realised, it becomes an issue.

The following risk management activities are more traditionally carried out by a Project Manager:
- Identify a risk
- Assess a risk
- Respond to a risk
- Reviewing risks

However, like most things in agile working environments, the responsibility for risk management is shared by all involved.

The old saying 'a problem shared is a problem halved' comes to mind. In agile software development environments, we accept that projects are ridden with complexity and uncertainty.

By promoting communication, distributing the responsibility of risk identification/mitigation and enabling ourselves to respond quickly to change, we are fundamentally better equipped to deal with risk than in more traditional environments.

With that said, there don't seem to be any official guidelines on how to manage risks within an agile environment, so here are a couple of techniques I've seen agile teams use.

The first is to draw a simple 2x2 grid on the team's whiteboard. The axes represent likelihood and impact. In other words, how likely is this risk to become an issue, and if it does, how big is the impact. When a risk is identified, the team writes it on a post-it note and sticks it in the relevant position on the grid. This prompts a discussion on what to do about it, especially if it goes in the top right, meaning it is highly likely and high impact.

In having this discussion, the aim really is to put the risk into one of two categories. Either to write a new task card for the team to take action and mitigate the risk in some way, or maybe a card to put contingency plans into place. Or they are simply made aware of it and agree not to worry about it, at least for now.

Another method I have seen is the ROAM method. ROAM stands for:
- Resolved
- Owned
- Accepted
- Mitigated

Again, you can use the team's whiteboard to good effect. Draw up 4 columns, one for each of the ROAM statuses above. When a risk is initially discussed, decide as a team what to do about it.

Resolved means that the risk is no longer a concern.

Owned means that someone has taken responsibility for doing something about it.

Accepted means that we accept we cannot do anything about this risk and we continue in the knowledge that it's there, but stop worrying about it.

Mitigated means that some action has been take to reduce the likelihood and/or impact.

Agile Portfolio Management

I recently read the book 'Agile Software Requirements' by Dean Leffingwell. I must admit, judging from the title, this is a book I wouldn't have picked up. Whilst there's always more to learn, I felt I knew enough about user stories and agile software requirements, at least for now!

But the book was recommended to me by Jim Highsmith when we were talking about Agile Programme and Portfolio Management. I was expressing a concern that I hadn't really stumbled across a really good source of information on that topic, and felt this was a bit of a gap in the agile books and materials currently available.

So on Jim's recommendation, I purchased and read Dean's book. And I'm very pleased I did!

Although I was already familiar with most of the concepts in the book, this is the first book I've read that really delivers such a comprehensive view of how to roll agile practices up to programme level and beyond that to project portfolio level. In my opinion it stops a bit short on the areas of project governance and the kinds of things an agile PMO might want to know, but it's certainly the most complete piece of work I've read in a long while.

One of my personal criticisms of agile books is that they are generally very specialised. In other words, each book is focused on a fairly narrow topic, so you have to read quite a lot of books to get a really good grasp of all the principles and practices. This is one book that I think you can read to get a really good overview of most agile techniques, regardless of specific methodology.

Better than that, for larger organisations, it provides some really good advice for how to scale agile practices up , from small, individual and independent teams, to larger inter-dependent programme teams, right the way up to unrelated portfolios of projects.

Lean

What is Lean?

Lean thinking is derived from the lean manufacturing methods pioneered by Toyota and Honda in the 1970's. Lean manufacturing is a process management philosophy that transformed the car manufacturer's approach to building vehicles.

The key principles behind Lean manufacturing were later translated into something more appropriate for Lean software development in a popular book by Tom and Mary Poppendieck. Tom and Mary's books, training, and talks at various agile conferences, have resulted in Lean software development becoming widely accepted within the agile community.

Lean software development has 7 key principles that are fundamental to the philosophy, but at the very heart of Lean thinking is principle #1, Eliminate Waste.

Agile development is a great example of Lean thinking in action. Agile methods are certainly Lean compared with the more traditional, documentation-intensive, waterfall approach to software development. But it's also possible to apply Lean thinking to agile methods. Perhaps there are some agile processes that could also be considered waste, certainly in some situations.

And so in the software development industry, Lean has also become somewhat synonymous with Kanban - the whiteboard system for tracking progress, which I'll explain more about later.

Kanban is extremely minimalist in terms of process. It's effectively Lean thinking applied to agile.

So Lean has a different set of principles to agile. But Lean principles are entirely complementary and I have found it advantageous to incorporate Lean thinking into my teams, even though they are already using agile development practices.

7 Key Principles of Lean Software Development

Before you can really put anything into practice, I think it's important first to understand the key principles.

So what are the 7 key principles of lean software development? They are:

1. Eliminate Waste
2. Build Quality In
3. Create Knowledge
4. Defer Commitment
5. Deliver Fast
6. Respect People
7. Optimise The Whole

In the following sections, I'll explain each of these Lean principles in turn, as concisely as I can and giving you my personal perspective on each.

Lean Principle #1 - Eliminate Waste

Lean software development advocates 7 lean principles, the first of which is Eliminate Waste. Sounds obvious really.

How many people came to work today to spend their time on waste? Some maybe! But not most. So what is waste, and how do you identify it?

Some waste is obvious. But other forms of waste are more difficult to spot or to solve. I'm sure in most organisations it's sometimes very difficult to identify what is waste and what is not. Some processes or conventions might seem wasteful, but actually provide real value elsewhere in the organisation, or prevent other forms of waste from emerging later. Other activities may seem valuable, but actually do not really result in any real value.

As I mentioned earlier, Lean development originated from lean manufacturing and the Toyota Production System in Japan. In these methods, they identified 3 general forms of waste, which they called in Japanese - 'Muda' (meaning unproductive), 'Mura' (unevenness, inconsistency) and 'Muri' (over-burden, unreasonableness).

In doing this, they also identified 7 particular types of waste:

- Over-production
- Unnecessary transportation
- Inventory
- Motion
- Defects
- Over-processing
- Waiting

In Lean software development, Tom and Mary Poppendieck translated these wastes into some things more specifically relevant to software development. For instance:

- Unnecessary code or functionality
- Starting more than can be completed
- Delay in the software development process
- Unclear or constantly changing requirements
- Bureaucracy
- Slow or ineffective communication
- Partially done work
- Defects and quality issues
- Task switching

As you know by now, a common agile development practice is the Retrospective, which is the process of the team meeting after each short iteration to discuss what went well, what didn't, and what could be done differently in the next iteration.

This iterative process of learning and continual improvement is an important part of identifying waste and eliminating it. In my experience this is one of the key benefits of agile software development.

Traditional software development and project management methods advocate a 'lessons learnt' process, but it generally takes place at the end of a project. By this time, things are forgotten, people have changed, the context has changed, and the team may be disbanding to move on to another project. As a result, the team may never really get a chance to put these learnings and changes into practice.

With agile development, these regular retrospectives enable the team to make small improvements regularly, and tackle changes in manageable, bite-sized pieces that can be actioned immediately.

Identifying and eliminating waste should not be a rare event conducted by process re-engineering consultants every few years. It should be a regular process, built into regular iterations, determined as much as possible by the team, and tackled in small, timely steps.

Making improvements little-and-often in this way creates a culture of continuous improvement - a learning environment - which for some organisations could potentially give you the edge over competitors.

So if you're not doing it already, I urge you to hold regular retrospectives. This is one agile development practice I can heartily recommend. Try to foster lively but healthy debate, critical but constructive feedback, and try to drive out meaningful and actionable improvements that actually help you to frequently identify and, more importantly, eliminate waste.

Lean Principle #2 - Build Quality In

Quality issues result in all sorts of waste. That's a fact. There's waste in testing the code more than once. Waste in logging defects. And waste in fixing them. As a result, Lean principles specifically seek to address this point.

The second principle of Lean Software Development is Build Quality In.

In agile methodologies such as Scrum and Extreme Programming (XP) - which personally I think are great examples of lean thinking in action - there are various practices to help you do this.

Firstly, there are quality assurance processes designed to avoid quality issues in the first place. Two examples of this are Pair Programming and Test Driven Development.

Pair Programming seeks to avoid quality issues by applying the minds of two developers to each task. The task benefits from the collective, combined experience of two developers instead of one, often resulting in better productivity as they see solutions that on their own they might not have done. Another positive outcome of Pair Programming is improved quality, since one person can be thinking slightly ahead of the other, catching issues before they occur.

Test Driven Development avoids quality issues by writing tests before writing code. In the simplest form, think about a Test Analyst/QA person writing down the test conditions for each feature just before it's developed. If the developer knows how it's going to be tested, they are much more likely to write code that addresses all the scenarios. In its more sophisticated form, Extreme Programming advocates stubbing out the code and writing automated unit tests for each of the test conditions before actually writing the code. The developer then writes the code to pass the tests.

Both of these practices come from Extreme Programming and both seek to prevent quality issues from occurring.

Constant Feedback - Inspect and Adapt

Both Scrum and XP build quality into the process in another way, which is inherent in many of the 10 key principles of agile software development. By doing development in small incremental steps, through close collaboration, and by developing in small iterations, these agile methods provide the opportunity for constant two-way feedback between the Product Owner and the team. This feedback can be immensely valuable, inspecting and adapting the product every single day in order to ensure the right level of quality - and most importantly of all - the right product.

Of course, the practices of XP and Scrum are completely complementary so it's possible to use both.

Minimise Time Between Stages

Another important technique for building quality into the development process is to minimise the time between development, testing and bug fixing. Rather than logging bugs, deal with them immediately. Logging bugs in a lot of cases is in fact waste. If the tester can test the code as soon as it's developed, and the developer can fix any bugs as soon as they are found, what is the value in logging them? On the other hand, a long gap between producing the code, testing it, and before fixing the bugs results in a loss of continuity. A loss in continuity that causes delays from task switching, knowledge gaps, and a lack of focus.

Frequent Integration

Most agile methods also advocate doing regular and frequent builds. At least daily, if not hourly. Extreme Programming advocates continuous integration, with code integrated into the overall system, built and automatically unit tested as soon as it is checked in. Minimising the gap between builds also reduces another form of waste, that is integration. On large waterfall projects, the integration and regression testing phases of the project can be very lengthy. Regular builds and frequent integration avoid that problem.

Automation

Agile development methods also encourage automated regression testing. Of course this is a practice that is not unique to agile development, but is another way to reduce the effort associated with finding quality issues before they occur in a live environment. This is admittedly the last stage, but quality assurance is built into every step in the process.

This is how Scrum and XP have translated Lean principles into practice in software development and how they have built quality into the process. In your own situation, you may also see other opportunities to build quality in.

Managing Trade-offs

One word of warning though. Quality is only one dimension of the project - the others being time, cost and scope. Sometimes there will be commercial reasons to trade-off quality against other factors, or to watch out for situations where attention to quality costs more than the issues you are trying to avoid.

One example of where agile methods acknowledge this in principle is the acceptance of rework ('refactoring') as a result of not having a detailed spec and complete design up-front. In traditional methodologies, these practices were designed to improve quality early in the project lifecycle. However, over many years, many people have found them to be counter-productive and hence agile methods were born.

Similarly, if you are working on fairly low-complexity visual components that have a low impact, it may be worth spending less time on quality assurance as the risk of quality issues occurring, and the impact if they do, is much lower. Naturally this is a judgement decision and unfortunately it can be very hard to know where to draw the line.

In summary...

Quality is obviously extremely important, or you inevitably create all sorts of waste further down the line. Build quality in. Build it in as early as possible in the process to avoid quality issues materialising. And build it in throughout the entire development process, not just at the end.

Lean Principle #3 - Create Knowledge

The third principle of lean software development is Create Knowledge.

This one seems a bit strange to me, as it almost seems obvious and common sense. But then I guess we all know that common sense isn't that common!

Thinking about the fact that the origins of Lean are in manufacturing, where the traditional approach is to simplify and standardise everything to the point where no knowledge is required, like on a factory line, then I guess it's clear why this principle was originally such a different way of thinking.

In software development, we all know that knowledge is paramount. We've all had situations where there's only one developer that can work on something, at least productively, or even at all. Nothing beats the knowledge that's created when someone actually writes the code.

Although I'm not particularly an advocate of Pair Programming, this is a specific agile practice from XP (Extreme Programming) that helps to ensure that the inherent knowledge that comes from writing the code is held by at least two people, rather than one.

So, if knowledge is important, and helps the longer term productivity and flexibility of the team, you need to take some specific actions in the short term and put some specific things in place to ensure that you create it.

Exactly what you do, as always, depends on your particular situation. Here are some things you could do on your projects to help create knowledge:

- Pair Programming
- Code reviews

- Documentation
- Wiki - to let the knowledge base build up incrementally
- Thoroughly commented code
- Knowledge sharing sessions
- Training
- Use tools to manage requirements/User Stories

I'm sure there are lots more. But these things are often not given the priority they really deserve. What do you do - proactively - to create knowledge in your teams?

Lean Principle #4 - Defer Commitment

Lean principle #4 is Defer Commitment.

I'm not sure I really like the name of this one. It could easily be misunderstood. It doesn't mean you should put off committing to anything indefinitely, or defer all decisions - that would obviously be a very bad idea.

What it does mean, is decide as late as possible, particularly for decisions that are irreversible, or at least will be impractical to reverse. Timebox critical decisions to be decided at the latest possible moment.

Obviously it is also important not too leave decisions too late. This can delay the team and make projects difficult. But, the later you can safely leave critical decisions, the more information you will have available to make the right decision when the time comes.

Deferring irreversible decisions means you keep your options open for as long as possible. By the time the decision needs to be made, there is every chance that you will know more about which of those options is the best route to take. It also gives you time to potentially explore the different options in more depth and experiment, helping to come to the right conclusion.

In areas of complexity or uncertainty, where things are very likely to change, this is especially important.

In areas like this, as well as deciding as late as possible, you should also try to architect your solution to be flexible, in order to make fewer decisions impractical to reverse.

Another example of deciding as late as possible in agile development methods is Sprint Planning, or iteration planning. In agile, you decide what features to include in each iteration and analyse them just in time for them to be developed.

Keeping decisions about features and the development of those features close together helps to ensure that the right product is delivered, because it leaves less room for change.

In more traditional project management methods, in between the specification and any particular features being developed, there is a much longer period of time when change can occur. Changes in requirements, changes to the underlying system, changes in technologies, changes in people (either the product owner or the development team), changes in direction, or of course changes in the market.

Deciding too early, you run the very likely risk that something significant will have changed, meaning your end product might meet the spec, but it might still be the wrong product! This is one reason why so many projects fail.

So, try (within reason) to architect your solution so that fewer commitments are irreversible. And defer commitment on irreversible decisions to the last responsible moment.

Lean Principle #5 - Deliver Fast

Deliver Fast. In a way, that's a funny principle to have. I would have thought that's stating the blinking obvious! But the reality is that it isn't. All too often in software development, things seem to take ages.

It is common for people to think too deeply about future requirements that may or may not ever arise.

It is common for people to be blocked - maybe requiring help or information from others - and not to react to that problem with the kind of urgency it deserves.

It is common to over-engineer solutions, both in terms of the software architecture, and also the business requirements.

Why build a simple solution and get it to market quickly to be enhanced incrementally based on real customer feedback when you can build one gigantic monolithic beast of a system and build it all before you launch anything for your users? (for those that can't detect sarcasm, that was meant to be ironic by the way!).

When a team is held up waiting for someone, others in the team could potentially pick up the task everyone is waiting for and get it done, even if it's not normally their role. It's important in agile teams to establish a good team spirit. It shouldn't be the case that everyone sticks rigidly to their job specs. "That's not my job" really isn't a phrase I'd ever like to hear in an agile team. If the team needs something done in order to achieve their objectives, the whole team should feel willing and able to help each other out, even if it sometimes means deviating from their usual speciality.

Speed to market is undoubtedly a competitive advantage. There is considerable evidence that companies who gain 'first mover advantage' go on to be the most successful companies in their chosen sphere. Companies can copy, and sometimes even come along later and do things better, but often it is the first to establish itself that wins the day and becomes the long term leader in its field.

Another advantage of delivering fast is that, if there is as little time as possible between the Product Owner stating the requirements and the team delivering the product, there is little chance of the requirements changing. Less time minimises the chances of changes in the market, changes in people, or even simply a change of mind.

So what is required to go faster?

Have the Right People

As with any methodology, it's important to have the right people. Lean thinking in the manufacturing industry originally changed the way companies think about their people. Instead of factory lines where the principle is to standardise everything to the extent that all people are performing small routine tasks and are essentially interchangeable, they moved towards the idea of having 'thinking people'. People who are able to think for themselves, solve problems, be proactive, be flexible, take appropriate actions, make decisions. As per Lean Principle #2 - Create Knowledge.

Keep It Simple

Another way to go faster, as I eluded to earlier, is to keep things simple. Keep the requirements simple. Keep the technical solution simple. Find the easiest way to meet the users' goals. Don't over-engineer. Don't spend too long considering future requirements that may never materialise. Get something simple to market and build on it based on real customer feedback.

Work as a Team

Really as a team, helping each other to make sure that the team achieves it's objectives, whatever it takes. Be flexible in the tasks you are willing to pick up. When you commit to something, do everything in your power to deliver on it.

Eliminate Waste

The first principle of Lean is to eliminate waste. Sometimes it's easier said than done, but this is clearly another way to deliver faster.

Build Quality In

And last but not least, in order to go faster, you really need to build quality in. A team that suffers from lots of bug fixing, or lots of breakages as changing one area affects another, or lots of post-delivery remediation work, can never go as fast as a team that is delivering good quality in the first place.

Lean Principle #6 - Respect People

Principle number 6 of Lean software development is Respect People.

It's yet another principle that should really be common sense. But unfortunately too many people sometimes forget this basic human courtesy, especially in the workplace. And all too often it's the most senior people that are the worst offenders.

Personally I think it's important to treat everyone with the same respect, whatever their job. It doesn't matter whether they're the CEO, a developer, project manager, the receptionist or the cleaner, respect everyone equally.

So, what does this actually mean in practice?

First of all, it means responding to people promptly, listening attentively, hearing their opinions and not dismissing them even when they are different to your own. It means encouraging people to have their say. Having empathy for their point of view and trying to see things from their perspective.

But, of course, it doesn't necessarily mean that you should always agree with them! That would be a very unhealthy situation. So one of the arts of respecting people is learning how to be assertive and disagree with a point of view, without sounding aggressive or threatening or just plain argumentative.

Another important part of respecting people is giving people the responsibility to make decisions about their work. To achieve this, it's important to build knowledge and develop people who can think for themselves. People who can think for themselves and are experts in their area often need to be empowered to feel respected.

But this in itself is a tricky area for many managers. How do you empower people enough, without losing control of the outcome?

One way is to make sure that the empowered person still communicates about their intended approach, and why they think it's the best approach. Then there is a chance to discuss pros and cons and understand why the person wants to take that particular decision. Questions can be asked to challenge whether or not someone has thought something all the way through, but can be asked in such a way to establish and maybe extend their own thinking, not to take over the solution or take the decision away from them, leaving them feeling disempowered and not in control.

Empowerment is particularly important with agile development methods. I wrote about this earlier in one of the 10 key principles of agile software development.

I think sometimes in the workplace this is easier said than done, which is why it isn't really just about common sense. Nevertheless, I think this principle is possibly one of the most important of all. Because the only way to be respected yourself, is to first respect others.

Lean Principle #7 - Optimise The Whole

The last of the 7 key principles of Lean software development is Optimise The Whole.

In their popular book, 'Implementing Lean Software Development', Mary and Tom Poppendieck explain that the software industry is legendary for its tendency to suboptimise. They give two examples:

Vicious circle number 1
A customer wants some new features 'yesterday'.
Developers hear: get it done fast, at all costs!
Result: sloppy changes are made to the code.
Complexity of the code base increases.
Number of defects in the code increases.
Future changes take longer.

Vicious circle number 2
Testing is overloaded with work.
Result: testing occurs a long time after the code is originally written, or testing is reduced.
Developers don't get immediate feedback, or some things are not properly tested.
There are more defects in the code.
Testers have more work.
Feedback to developers and quality improvements are delayed further.
Changes take longer.

These vicious circles can ultimately result in an exponential increase in the time it takes to add new features. They can also result in a notably lower quality product, which affects the end users and ultimately may also affect their efficiency or the competitiveness of the product.

A Lean organisation seeks to optimise the whole value stream, not just individual functions or teams. It is common for big delays in projects and processes - as well as communication issues and misunderstandings leading to other problems - to be caused by handoffs between teams, departments or organisations. Crossing organisational boundaries - even internal ones - is expensive.

One of the principles of agile methods that has resulted from this experience is the idea that the best way to organise teams is so they are complete, multi-disciplined, co-located product teams that have all the roles and skills they need to deliver a request from start to finish, without reference to other teams.

Naturally this can be hard to achieve - particularly if you don't have the authority to re-structure your organisation! That's one of the reasons why sometimes it's important that agile adoption is driven from the top.

Nevertheless, the fact remains that many of the issues we face in traditional IT departments are caused by structuring teams around roles or skills, rather than products or projects.

When a team is organised by product, with everything it needs to deliver, there are some distinct advantages. Apart from optimising the team's workflow and avoiding some of the issues mentioned above, I have also observed across many teams that when organised like this teams have better ownership of the products they are responsible for, leading to better commitment, quality and innovation. They also tend to have a stronger sense of team spirit and greater cooperation between team members, as the team is one team with shared goals.

Putting all of this together with the better optimised workflow, the benefits of organising in this way can be extremely significant - not only in terms of the team's performance, but also in terms of the quality of the product, which ultimately can make your organisation more competitive. And better products can have a direct impact on the bottom line, either by improving internal efficiency, or by earning more revenue from products.

Less is the New More!

There is no doubt that Lean is increasingly popular in the software development industry; certainly within the agile community anyway.

But how does it fit in with agile, and more specifically, how does it really fit in with agile methods like Scrum and Extreme Programming (XP)?

I mentioned before that Lean software development shares many, if not all, of the key principles of agile software development. As a result, in can potentially be seen as an instance of agile, much like Scrum is another instance and Extreme Programming is another.

Whilst Scrum focuses on agile management practices, and XP focuses more on agile engineering practices, Lean software development is an extension of the underlying principles and has a sharp focus on eliminating waste.

It can also be seen the other way around, that agile is an instance of Lean thinking.

It's certainly true that agile principles and methods eliminate a lot of waste, especially in comparison with previous project management methods and traditional waterfall projects. That's for sure.

And it's also true that agile - starting with the original agile manifesto - has its roots in Lean manufacturing, as pioneered by Toyota and Honda.

But Lean thinking can actually be applied to any methodology, whether it's waterfall, Scrum, Extreme Programming, or whatever.

For example, in Scrum, is Sprint Planning waste? It's certainly very time-consuming, although I would argue it's not generally waste. There can potentially be enormous value in aligning the whole team, unifying the team on common goals, establishing a common understanding of what needs to be done, and committing as a team. On the other hand, in some circumstances, when the work is nigh-on impossible to plan and Sprints are routinely disrupted, Sprint Planning can potentially be a big waste of time.

As another example, this time in XP - is Pair Programming waste? There are some circumstances where Pair Programming is extremely valuable, for instance, when one person is learning from another, to spread knowledge about areas of the code, and to increase quality. On the other hand, if these are not particularly issues for your team, and if the tasks are relatively straightforward, it could certainly be argued that Pair Programming is waste.

It's no wonder people find this all a bit confusing! So what are you meant to make of all this?

My personal suggestion is this...

For those adopting agile development principles, it can certainly be valuable to adopt some common practices, such as Scrum or Extreme Programming to bring some structure and process to the principles and help the team to put the principles into practice.

But in adopting these practices, or any other practices for that matter, you could also benefit from Lean thinking. Think hard about your particular circumstances, and whether any of your processes are really waste? If they are, regardless of methodology, you should really try to eliminate them.

One word of caution though. Be sure you really understand the intrinsic value of any process before you eliminate it. Sometimes the benefits are soft and not immediately obvious. Until you really understand the principles, and have practical experience of why they work, you're in no place to adapt them. Agile practices are meant to be adaptive, but only when you're ready - be careful not to throw the baby out with the bathwater!

Kanban

What is Kanban? Like Scrum and Extreme Programming (XP), it's a method for managing software development and other processes, but by comparison it is fairly minimalist with a heavy emphasis on visual tracking and just-in-time delivery.

Like agile methods and lean principles, Kanban is also derived from just-in-time manufacturing pioneered by Toyota, and has been adapted for use on software development projects. Here is a brief overview of what it is...

The name Kanban originates from Japanese and translates roughly as "signboard" or "billboard". It has 5 core properties:

1. Visualise the workflow
A common way to visualise the workflow is to use a whiteboard or card wall to track work. Columns are drawn up to represent the process stages the work goes through, and post-it notes or cards are used to represent units of work (often as User Stories or tasks). An example of the columns in a software development process might typically be: Analysing, Developing, Testing, Done. In its simplest form, the columns might just be To Do, Doing and Done. As cards progress through the workflow, they are moved from column to column to keep track of their progress and to highlight where everything is in an extremely visible way.

2. Limit WIP (Work In Progress)
The concept of limiting Work In Progress is that it's a 'pull' system, rather than 'push'. There is no point pushing more work into the next stage of the process than can really be handled. Setting WIP limits creates an artificial limitation to stimulate discussion about how to improve the flow of work through the system. Work is only pulled into the next stage when there is capacity to do it.

3. Manage Flow

In Kanban, there is a heavy emphasis of managing flow and maximising throughput, ensuring that the flow of work through each stage is monitored, measured and reported. The aim is to try to create a continuous flow, where all the work is flowing seamlessly through the process until it reaches the end, without stalling and without creating long queues for subsequent stages.

4. Make Process Policies Explicit

Until a process policy is made explicit, it is hard to have a conversation about how to improve it. Examples from Toyota's original just-in-time manufacturing are:

- Do not send defective products to the subsequent process
- The subsequent process only withdraws what is needed
- Produce only the exact quantity withdrawn by the subsequent process

5. Improve Collaboratively

Kanban advocates continuous improvement through a series of small incremental changes, so improvement is evolutionary and more likely to stick. Ideas for improvement are discussed regularly and the team agrees changes that it would like to try out. This reduces resistance to change and increases the ability to experiment with new ideas.

Kanban does not prescribe a specific set of roles or process steps. That's why Kanban can be used so easily in conjunction with your existing processes, whatever they might be. That's why it works equally well within Scrum or in combination with XP's engineering practices as it does on its own.

In my experience, it is common practice to use a Kanban system as part of Scrum and XP. However it is often only the whiteboard or card wall element that is used and people using Kanban more fully have a much heavier emphasis on limiting WIP and maximising flow.

270

Using Kanban to manage the software development process without any of the engineering practices in XP, like Scrum, is unlikely to yield any major benefits in terms of software quality. However, also like Scrum, it is likely to result in some significant benefits in terms of visibility, tracking, maximising throughput and continuous learning - things that are immensely valuable in themselves. If these are your hotspots, Kanban is an interesting method for you to think about.

So what's the fundamental difference between Kanban and Scrum when you think about it at a high level. Scrum is based on short, fixed length iterations and has a lot more ceremony built into it, for instance Sprint Planning, Daily Standups, Retrospectives, etc. Whereas Kanban does not run in iterations. Instead it's a continuous flow of work and the focus is on how to get each unit of work through the process as fast as possible, with little emphasis on up-front planning.

Because of these differences, I have seen teams successfully apply Kanban instead of Scrum in areas that are unplannable. For instance, in an infrastructure team where they are responding to tickets raised by other teams and the demand is not predictable or controllable. Or a Commercial Solutions team where they are responding to advertiser demands and the team has no control over the demand from third parties. In these cases, I have found that Kanban can deliver many of the benefits of Scrum, with lower overheads and without feeling that your Sprints are constantly disrupted.

On the other hand, I have also found that the use of Kanban on its own on a major project provided less predictability in terms of really understanding the team's capacity (or velocity) and therefore predicting the end date was very hard and the project over-ran significantly. In our case, we found ways to mitigate this by combining it with some elements of XP and Scrum, but I wouldn't personally start with Kanban on its own on a large project. I would be more inclined to learn how to apply it and refine it on BAU (business as usual) and then use it on projects when you have mastered how to better predict your cycle times.

For example, here is a simple way for novice users of Kanban to create more predictability:

- Use User Stories still to capture and represent each unit of work.

- Quickly put a points value on each User Story in order to get an approximate understanding of its size and to break it down as small as possible.

- Without working in iterations, at the end of the week count how many points are in the Done column on the board. This is the team's weekly velocity and helps you to understand the team's capacity.

- Based on this, you can estimate the likely time it will take for stories in the queue to be done.

Maximising Flow: Work-In-Progress Limits

One of the key concepts of Lean is the idea of flow, i.e. how to keep things moving in one continuous flow. By contrast, a common problem in agile software development is bottlenecks that hold up the team's progress during a Sprint or iteration.

In traditional waterfall projects, everything happens in sequence, so this bottleneck does not occur because it is planned in. For instance, the testing starts when all the development is complete.

However, in agile software development projects, the analysis, design, development, testing, etc are all happening in parallel during a Sprint, with the team's efforts converging on completed features in a short time period; perhaps as short as 1 or 2 weeks.

If you have specialist roles in your team, for instance designers, analysts or testers, this can inevitably create bottlenecks, where the developers are waiting for visuals from designers, or testers are waiting for completed code from developers, or the release is waiting for testers to complete their QA.

A common bottleneck, at least in my experience, is for teams to develop more features than can be tested properly by the end of the Sprint, meaning that testing is the bottleneck and the release is delayed.

So what's the solution?

The easy answer - of course - is to make sure you have enough people, particularly in the more specialist roles, so there is always enough slack in the schedule to complete a Sprint without these bottlenecks occurring. But in reality, the chances of the balance always being perfect (for every type of work you ever do) is low, so some bottlenecks are sometimes inevitable. And in these challenging economic times, what do you do when adding resources simply isn't an option?

One solution, coming from Lean practices, is the concept of Work-In-Progress, or Work-In-Play limits; a concept borrowed from Toyota's practice of lean manufacturing.

This concept supports one of my 10 Key Principles of Agile Software Development, where I write about completing each feature before moving on to the next, making sure features are shippable at the end of a Sprint.

The idea of WIP limits is to try to ensure that you never start or complete a task that cannot be passed smoothly on to the next stage without blocking up the 'factory line'. To do this means having a 'pull system' rather than a 'push system' and is intended to create a smooth continuous flow of work down the line.

For example, if a classic (and simplified) software development lifecycle is develop and test, testers would pull features from development when they are ready and have capacity to test. Developers would not push completed features to testers whether the tester is ready or not.

This is a simple concept, but like many things in agile software development, it's different to what we've all been used to for so many years, so it takes a little thinking about!

So let's say you set a WIP limit that no more than 3 features can be in play at any one time. You have 3 slots on the board for development, and 3 slots for testing. What happens when the testing slots are all full and the developers have capacity to do more?

If they think the tester will be done before they complete the 4th feature, they can safely start it. But what if they think they can complete the 4th feature before the tester is done? What should they do? Should they sit idle?

Maybe they could complete it and not check it in to the central source code until a testing slot is available. That's okay, but you certainly don't want your developers racing ahead of the tester and creating a pile of backlogged features that aren't checked in.

Maybe they should do some other task? (for instance update documentation, or research a tricky feature coming up). Not a bad option if they need doing, but you really don't want to invent work that isn't necessary.

Personally, my preferred option is to help with the testing to clear a feature so the team can move on? Then the flow of work can continue, and the team is much more likely to reach a stage of completeness at the end of the Sprint, without the tester being overloaded and the release eventually being delayed.

If you do opt for this approach, make sure developers don't test their own work, if at all possible, and have your tester still play a QA role and guide any testing that's being done by others.

There was an interesting debate about WIP limits between two of the heavyweight thinkers of the agile community. Alistair Cockburn has been commenting on Twitter that WIP limits are for beginners, referring to them as 'training wheels'. Whilst David Anderson argues on his blog that WIP Limits are for Adults too!

What do I think about this debate? Certainly many parts of agile development are common sense. But we all know that lots of people don't have common sense. And that in software development there are often many variables and keeping focus on something like this can be very difficult without some simple rules and guidelines for people to work to. That's why agile works. Because it's simple.

If Work-In-Play limits help some teams to keep focus on this key principle, help to start the right conversations when there are bottlenecks, and ultimately therefore help to ensure work is completed at the end of a Sprint, then I'm all for it.

Perhaps a more mature agile team might impose WIP limits temporarily on occasions when they can see that work is in danger of piling up at one stage of the lifecycle. In this case, WIP limits could be a useful tool to ensure the team has a complete feature set at the end of the Sprint, and not, for instance, a load of untested features.

"Take The Time To Write A Short Letter"

It's a funny old saying. I'm sure you've heard it before. Allegedly, Mark Twain once said, "I didn't have time to write a short letter, so I wrote a long one instead".

I think it's very true. It takes a lot longer to cut something down. To distil the same value into relatively few words. A lot more.

I couldn't help thinking that the same is true of code.

And process.

Keeping things simple can be complicated. But I'm sure it's worth it.

P.S. This page took me ages ;)

Do Less

A key mantra in Lean thinking is 'Do Less'.

There is overhead, and therefore waste, in task switching. And there is also more value in delivering something earlier, rather than progressing multiple things and having them all partially complete and taking longer to finish.

Here is a simple example of why it pays to do less...

Let's say you have 3 projects. Each project takes 3 months effort to complete. Each project delivers a value of $10,000 in month 1, increasing by $10,000 each month until it plateaus at $50,000 per month.

Scenario 1 is that all 3 projects are progressed in parallel, which is what usually happens, especially in larger organisations. No value would be realised until the end of 9 months. In reality it might also take longer than that, due to the inefficiency of task switching.

Scenario 2 is that you complete each of the projects in turn, concentrating fully on each project until it is finished. After month 3, project 1 starts accumulating value. After month 6, project 2 starts delivering value. After month 9, project 3 is also delivered, no later than in the previous scenario.

Using this simple example, cumulatively we have managed to achieve a lot more value in scenario 2 where each project is completed in turn. We also have the benefit of faster speed to market for the first 2 projects, which could potentially give us the edge over our competitors and allow us to establish our market position first.

Now let's look at the numbers for year 1:

- Scenario 1 accumulates benefits of $180,000
- Scenario 2 accumulates benefits of $610,000

That's a massive difference by any standards! Over 330% more value.

It's such a simple concept. And logically it's undebatable really. But we all seem to fall into the same common trap. The trap that we need to show everyone progress, so we end up doing too much at once, even if it delivers less value overall for our organisation.

Maybe this explanation might help you to convince others.

Don't believe me? Here are the numbers:

If You Chase Two Rabbits, You Won't Catch Either

Need I say more?

No, thought not.

Agile Teams

One Team

One of the key principles of agile development, and in particular Scrum, is the concept of "One Team".

The team should include all key roles for the product, wherever they report to, including Product Owner, Product Manager, Test Analyst, Developers, Business Analysts, and any others that might be appropriate such as SEO, Creative, User Research, etc.

For agile to work effectively, all team members need to be included in Sprint Planning when the requirements are discussed. And they need to be informed, either at Scrums or as they happen, about any clarifications or changes to requirements when they occur.

Using an agile approach, collaboration between team members becomes a critical success factor. Without a full specification, agile requirements are barely sufficient and collaboration is the key to success.

It is imperative, therefore, that all team members are included in all key aspects of your regular Scrum process. Irrespective of line management boundaries, which may well be different, it's imperative that the Scrum team is acting as one.

Another example of One Team is what happens when a team member is blocked. Or one role in the team is overloaded. For instance when the testing is overloaded, as is often the case. In a situation like this, there's little point in the developers continuing to produce more untested code. It would be more effective to help with the testing and get something finished inside the iteration.

Another similar example is where the analysts can't go fast enough to feed the developers. In which case the developers can do some analysis to help the team move faster as a whole.

In agile development, it's not so much about sticking rigidly to your own job description and specialisation, but more about how every team member can help the team to achieve its objective.

One last example is the way IT and business people often act as though they are separate organisations. IT people are referred to as 'resources' and business people as 'the business', as though they work for completely different companies. Agile seeks to break down this unhealthy customer/supplier or us and them attitude, and instead seeks to focus the team on a shared purpose, creating a strong team spirit and a real feeling of being One Team.

Agile Teams Need To Pull Together

Sometimes, agile teams have to be literally just that.

Some agile methods - such as Scrum and Extreme Programming - advocate team members that are multi-skilled and able to tackle almost any task. That is, teams of generalists; developers that can write code, and can also do analysis and testing and whatever other tasks are required.

In principle, this is a good concept because:

- A team of generalists never suffers from any bottlenecks, where the team is waiting on someone with particular skills.

- As a manager of a team of generalists, you don't have to try to work out the ideal profile of the team, anticipating in advance how many developers, testers, analysts, etc you'll need at any given stage of the product's development. This is challenging anyway, and changes over time.

However, in reality, setting up with teams of generalists is not always possible. And not necessarily ideal.

Many organisations already have specialists. For instance, designers, front-end developers, back-end developers, database administrators, business analysts, testers, project managers, product managers, etc. Unless you want to get rid of these specialists, and employ only developers, you need to put these people to work and you will definitely benefit from their specialist expertise.

And generalists that have all the required skills are rather hard to find!

You might find a developer that is really good at both front-end and back-end development. You might find a developer that can also do analysis. You might even find a developer that thinks like a tester.

Although this one can be difficult, because we all know that most developers can't test for toffee! And, if you are lucky enough to find someone who really is good at all of these things, what are the chances of them also being good at UI/graphic design?!

Maybe. But in my experience, generally not.

So what do you do?

Personally, I think you need a team with all of these skills. It's a multi-disciplinary team by virtue of the fact that the team has all of these skills. Not because everyone in the team has all of these skills.

If you can find generalists, to minimise the number of specialists and reduce potential bottlenecks, great! Combining some roles can certainly help with this.

For instance - in my experience of agile - the roles of analyst and tester can potentially be merged into the role of Test Analyst. And the more generalised role of Product Manager might combine the traditional roles of Project Manager and Business Analyst, as well as introducing some important product management disciplines.

But in the end you will probably need some specialists.

In which case, it is very important for these specialists to be flexible. To be agile. In the true sense of the word.

You might be called a Tester, and might specialise in testing, but you should be prepared to help with analysis and any other tasks that you have the skills to do. You might be called a Developer, and specialise in development, but you should be prepared to test your colleagues' work if it's testing that the team really needs to get done. You might be called a Project Manager, and specialise in project management, but you should be prepared to help with analysis and testing if it helps the team to deliver.

This is, of course, a question of attitude. There's no place for "jobsworths" in an agile team. In an agile team, you never want to hear that "it's not in my jobspec". It's a question of team spirit. Completing your own tasks while the team fails to deliver is not success. Not for a team player. The team succeeds, or fails, as a team.

Co-location

As per usual in agile development, most things are not black or white, they are shades of grey. I don't think the co-location debate is any different.

I've read plenty of articles and blog posts about the merits of co-location. Mostly I would strongly agree. I've also read lots about how co-location is an essential ingredient of agile development. But I've also read some very good counter-arguments explaining how agile can work - and is working - with teams that are not located together and working effectively across borders.

I think the debate, as with most things depends on your circumstances.

In my experience, I have often had business teams in multiple locations. So is it best to locate the associated development teams in the same building as the business units, or in a central development group co-located with their technical peers and other people of a like mind?

There is certainly a case for colocation with either group, but they can't be in two places at once so sometimes we just have to choose!

In situations like this, I think it comes down to which group of people is most valuable to collaborate with most frequently.

If you have an established product or business in a BAU (Business-As-Usual) situation, but a development team whose development practices are not well established, I would suggest that ongoing product development is best placed near other, more established development teams, where good development practices and experience can be more easily shared amongst peers.

If, on the other hand, you have an established development team with good development practices, performing well and delivering what's expected, but a product or business unit that is not in a stable situation (e.g. new product development, competitive threat, major problems, etc), I would suggest that co-location with the Product Owner (and maybe business units) is much more important. In this case, active user involvement is imperative, in order to provide extra visibility, get very regular feedback and customer insight, and be able to respond accordingly.

In any event, I do think distance adds complexity and risk. If the opportunity for face-to-face communication is virtually nil, then I think the compromise is a really big one, so I strongly recommend co-location wherever it's possible.

Agile Teams Need Managers Too!

Some exponents of agile say the agile teams do not need managers. Whilst it is true that a managers role changes in an agile environment, I personally think that agile teams need managers too!

Organisations need managers, for a wide variety of reasons. And let's face it, the roles of Product Owner and Scrum Master in agile methodologies are management roles.

They may not be management roles in the traditional sense, but management roles they are.

The Product Owner is there to manage stakeholders, manage incoming requests and prioritise work for the team. This is management.

The Scrum Master, or Iteration Manager, is there to deal with any issues that are impeding the team's progress, facilitate communication, orchestrate the process, etc. This is also management.

What Scrum has effectively done is to split the traditional management role into two, one with a focus on aligning the team's activities with the goals of the business; the other with a focus on the internal organisation of the team.

The aspects of management these roles don't explicitly address are duties relating to line management, for example:

- Reporting up the line
- Setting budgets and managing finances
- Managing the performance of individuals in the team
- Developing people's careers
- Ensuring compliance with important company policies or regulations

- Setting out a clear vision and strategy for the future
- Understanding the wider organisational context and identifying opportunities and constraints
- 'Selling' the team's achievements and goals within the wider organisation
- Raising funds for projects
- Signing off and managing holidays, sickness, expenses, invoices, etc - i.e. the administrative side of management
- Deciding on the most appropriate organisational structure
- Hiring and firing

And I'm sure there are many others!

So I guess one possibility is that the traditional management role was always too big for some people. To fulfill all of these responsibilities, and those of the Scrum Master, and those of the Product Owner, and by the way to be the assigned leader. Management, done right, is a big deal and it's why anyone who has tried it knows it's not easy.

Scrum alleviates this challenge by splitting the management role, spreading the responsibilities and making the challenge of management more achievable.

The Product Owner can worry about what the team should be doing. The Scrum Master can worry about the internal process and making sure issues are being addressed. And line managers can worry about all the other stuff!

Having said that, a key principle of agile methods is that agile teams must be empowered.

Agile methods advocate the idea of self-organising teams. In a way that's quite funny, because the responsibilities of the Scrum Master and Product Owner mean that in many ways Scrum teams are far from self-organising!

Nevertheless, the idea is that whilst the process may be somewhat prescribed by Scrum and managed by the Scrum Master, the team will make most decisions about how things should be done for themselves, and will pick their tasks rather than having them allocated by a manager.

In any case, self-organisation is not boundaryless!

Regardless of all this, like any other teams, agile teams still need leadership. Leadership sometimes comes from one of these management roles, as managers often end up as managers because they have some level of leadership skills. Sadly, sometimes they don't! Other times leadership comes from within the team, which is equally good and in my opinion should be encouraged.

Leaders can be appointed (e.g. line managers, Scrum Master, Product Owner), or they can be emergent leaders that emerge naturally because of their skills, expertise or personality, rather than because they've been formally assigned a leadership role.

Wherever it comes from, leadership is probably the difference between good teams and great teams! Inspirational leadership can transform a team's energy, and therefore their ability to overcome obstacles, strive for bigger goals, and bond as a team.

20 Simple Things You Can Do
To Boost Your Agile Career

Here are 20 simple things you can do to boost your agile development career. Of course they are not unique to agile methods. But agile development is so dependent on people, collaboration and teamwork that these qualities will probably help you even more in an agile environment than they might have done before. Here they are...

1. Take responsibility
2. Do what you say you will
3. Help others
4. Respect everyone equally
5. Be positive
6. Embrace change
7. Suggest improvements
8. Pay attention to detail
9. Have pride in your work
10. Work hard
11. Be knowledgeable
12. Share your knowledge
13. Stay professional
14. Be flexible
15. Do whatever it takes
16. Be honest
17. Be modest
18. Praise others
19. Be happy
20. Be yourself

A Fool With A Tool Is Still A Fool!

There are many tools that can potentially help to manage agile development. Of course it's important in any approach to have good tools, but in my view the process is much more important than the tools you use to support it. And even more important than that - by far - is the mindset of the people applying the process.

Agile development turns the traditional development approach completely on its head. So it's of paramount importance that all people involved adopt the agile mindset. Otherwise you're in grave danger, because a fool with a tool is still a fool.

Agile Teams At Full Stretch

In my experience, most developers are over-optimistic and tend to under-estimate.

However it's not uncommon for some teams to estimate on the cautious side. If you find yourself in this situation and finishing the Sprint early, include a couple of "stretch tasks" (or features/stories from the next Sprint).

It's important to specifically identify them as stretch tasks. Make sure noone is ever beaten up if no stretch tasks are ever achieved in the Sprint. By contrast, do make sure you celebrate as a team if you reach any stretch tasks - even if it's just a lot of back slapping and self congratulation!

And don't forget to apply the same rules to the stretch tasks as everything else; they must be 100% complete (i.e. shippable) to count.

Old Habits Die Hard

In agile development, it's easy to develop bad habits!

Or to have trouble kicking old habits.

For example:

- Daily stand-ups not every day
- Daily stand-ups not involving anyone from the business side of things
- Mini waterfalls in iterations
- Little to nothing quite completed at the end of the iteration
- Pressing too hard for increased velocity
- Team Leaders taking over team responsibilities
- People leaving things to each other

I've certainly seen all of these bad habits in action.

The truth is, there's not really a specific remedy for these things, except what's already built in to the agile principles and methodologies. So really it's just a case of understanding why these issues are bad, and making sure the team has good professional discipline.

That's partly the role of Scrum Master in Scrum; helping to ensure that the team follows the basic principles and processes, and making sure that any decision not to do these things is at least a conscious one.

Agile Games - Ball Point Game

For those of you that believe in learning through play, the ball point game (invented I believe by Boris Gloger) is one game I can heartily recommend.

I recently had the privilege of working independently with one of London's top media companies and helping them to rejuvenate their agile roots.

I ran an all-day workshop as a refresher on agile principles and practices and as a warm-up exercise I played this game.

I was really happy with the results.

The group seemed to have such a lot of fun doing it, which got everyone into a relaxed and participative frame of mind, and there were so many interesting parallels with agile and lean that it provided a really useful basis for reflection and discussion.

I played the game with about 50 people in a large meeting space. The room was large but it wasn't enormous, and it worked well despite the large size of the group.

To play the game, you will need a lot of balls, if you'll forgive the expression! I found that tennis balls worked well and I had 60 balls for a group of 50 people. You will also need a stopwatch, and a flipchart and pen.

Here is how it works...

The object of the game is to pass as many balls as possible through the team in 2 minutes. There are relatively few rules, but they must be adhered to. These are effectively the team's constraints. Here they are:

- If you've played this game before, please participate silently so you don't spoil it for others.
- You are one big team - you cannot change your team size.
- Every team member must touch each ball for it to count.
- As each ball is passed between team members, it must have air time, i.e. it must not be passed directly from hand to hand.
- You cannot pass the ball to the person immediately to your left or right.
- If you drop a ball, you cannot pick it up.
- There will be a penalty (points deducted) if you break any of the rules.
- Every ball must end where it started. For each ball that does, the team scores 1 point.

You have 2 minutes to self-organise as a team and plan your approach. One person from the group will write on the flipchart an estimate of how many balls the team thinks it can do.

You will then play the game for 2 minutes. At the end of the game, you will record on the flipchart how many balls the team actually managed to do, alongside their original estimate.

You will then spend 1 minute learning how to improve, making a note of what the team has decided to change on the flipchart next to the estimate and actual.

Then do it again.

In all, you will do 5 iterations, recording the estimate, actual and changes each time.

It was really fascinating to watch how the team self-organised, how they communicated, and to observe where the leadership came from and in what style. It was also really interesting to see how the team learned, and how their estimates became more accurate until they changed the process.

The key lesson here is that all processes have a natural velocity. To speed things up, it is often not a case of individuals working harder or faster, but a case of changing the process.

Some of the other parallels with agile or lean, and some of the questions worth posing to the team, are:

- What happened? Which iteration felt best? Why?
- Were improvements achieved by working harder or faster?
- What were there bottlenecks? How were they identified?
- How well did the team self-organise?
- Were interjections of experience (from person running the game) useful? If so, even self-organising teams should take guidance from people with relevant experience
- The game had a natural rhythm and flow, like continuous flow advocated in lean thinking
- People were not disturbed during the process
- The 'pull system' maximises flow - no point throwing balls to someone who isn't ready to catch them
- The team had a shared goal and was focused on a common purpose
- Face to face communication - would it have worked as well if communication was by phone or by email?
- Would it have helped to document the process?
- The power of the retrospective - concept of 'fail fast' and learning quickly as a team
- Shows the idea of sprints or iterations, where the team goes through repeated cycles of plan, do, review, ...
- Where did the leadership come from? In what style?
- Using the number of points as a simple measure of the team's results, did the estimate and actual start to converge? (until the process was changed)

During the game, you may need to give some hints to help the team learn in such short, limited timeframes. Try not to make the hints too obvious too early in the game.

For instance, after a couple of iterations, during the learning minute, you might want to give the team clues, such as eliminate waste, maximise resources. Later you might want to hint that they should use both hands, and later still that they could cup heir hands together to drop fewer balls (less waste).

I played this game for a second time and it was also interesting to see that both times in the first iteration, the teams neglected to put any system in place to count their score and measure their output. As a result, they had no idea how well they'd done and if they didn't put this right, they would have no way of telling whether their changes were really effective. I thought that was a great way of demonstrating the value of velocity and measurement.

All in all, it was a great ice-breaker, was good fun and was very thought-provoking. Later in the day, people regularly referred back to concepts demonstrated by the game.

Agile Practices Are Meant To Be Adaptive

Many people have commented or written about which agile practices really define 'being agile'. What's more important than the practices is the key agile principles behind them.

Whichever methodology you prefer, whichever practices you adopt, and whichever you don't, the most important thing is to understand these principles, and adapt your practices according to the needs of your team and the needs of your organisation. That, for me, is really the essence of agile. It's adaptive. Not prescriptive.

The problem, however, is that people whose understanding of the principles is not necessarily that deep might adjust the practices and lose much of the value. I've certainly seen this.

Ken Schwaber raises this very point in his book 'Agile Software Development with Scrum'. Until you really understand the principles, and have practical experience of <u>why</u> the process works, you are in no position to adapt it.

That's where a prescriptive approach works well for teams in the early stages of adoption. And why methods such as Scrum, Extreme Programming, and others, really do help teams to get started and find success.

Only once the key agile principles are truly embedded - not the processes, but in the mindset of the team - can the team really become truly agile, and learn the art of adapting the right things at the right time.

Definition of DONE! 10 Point Checklist

A key principle of agile software development is "done means DONE!"

To be more specific, here's an example of a 10-point checklist of what might constitute 'feature complete':

1. Code produced.
2. Code commented, checked in and run against current version in source control.
3. Peer reviewed (or produced with pair programming) and meeting development standards.
4. Builds without errors
5. Unit tests written and passing.
6. Deployed to system test environment and passed system tests.
7. Passed UAT (User Acceptance Testing) and signed off as meeting requirements by the Product Owner.
8. Any build/deployment/configuration changes implemented, documented, communicated, automated
9. Relevant documentation/diagrams produced or updated
10. Product Backlog updated

The definition of done is something that should be defined collectively by the team to suit the team's own needs and circumstances. But hopefully this list gives you a useful starting point for the discussion.

Pair Programming - An Extremely Agile Practice

Pair Programming. It's probably one of the most extreme practices of Extreme Programming (XP). It's an area of agile software development that polarises opinion.

The concept is simple enough. Two developers work side by side on the same piece of work, sharing a keyboard and screen and working together to produce the code.

The main advantage of pair programming is usually cited as improving quality, which also improves productivity further down the line.

Another advantage is spreading knowledge, as at least two people will know each area of the system. And it can also help with skills development - a kind of coaching and mentoring technique with one of the pair potentially being more experienced than the other.

It's also possible to benefit from the theory that two brains are better than one. A simple way of explaining this is that two people have very different experiences. One may see a solution that the other doesn't. It's possible that two minds might lead to solutions that are quicker to implement and simpler to maintain.

Even without pair programming, it's quite common for two developers to work together when they hit a particularly thorny problem. It's usually a little while before someone declares they are stuck and asks for help. With pair programming, this situation doesn't really arise, so time is not lost with single developers persevering for too long on their own.

The other area it can help with is motivation and retaining focus. Someone is much less inclined to become distracted and spend time on Facebook, for instance, when they are working with a colleague.

The motivation advantage reminds me of DIY in my case. I hate DIY! I will put it off for as long as possible. I'm simply not interested enough, so it doesn't get done. My solution to this? Invite my father-in-law round!

Once he's in, I have to get it done because that's why he came over. He gets me started and keeps me focused.

Hopefully you don't have wide-spread motivation problems in your team, or you have deeper problems to worry about! But we all go through short periods like this, and pair programming keeps them to a minimum.

On the other hand, pair programming also has some disadvantages.

In the short-term, there is a loss of productivity, or at least perceived productivity. You have to have sufficient budget to put two developers on each piece of work. If your team needs specialist skills, you have to have a team where there are at least two people with each major skillset. And when you need to hire another person, you ideally need to hire in pairs.

I think it's also important that the team members have the right chemistry. That they spark off each other, rather than spark each other off! It's important they can work very closely together without differing opinions causing endless frustration.

There's a loss of autonomy, having to explain everything and constantly build consensus with your pair. Sometimes you'll be constrained by your partner; other times they may be going too fast for you.

This reminds me of back-seat drivers. It's so annoying when someone sitting beside you keeps interfering and just won't let you drive how you want to! It's tiring and frustrating.

These are important soft-factors that can make or break pair programming in practice.

In the end then, like many agile development practices, you have to look at the unique circumstances of your team, and understanding these factors, decide for yourself when and if to adopt pair programming.

Take Responsibility

I had an interesting conversation with a colleague about a situation where an obviously important feature was missed, and the reason given was that it wasn't specified in the requirements.

If I arrange to meet you somewhere at a particular time, I don't expect to have to tell you how to get there. I don't expect to write down the route for you. I don't expect to write down alternative routes in case there's something wrong with the preferred route. I don't tell you what mode of transport to use. I don't check the weather forecast and let you know what you should wear.

You figure all that out for yourself.

I just expect to see you there, unless you run into problems that delay you, in which case please let me know so you don't leave me standing around in the rain wondering when you might arrive!

Obviously it's okay to ask questions. Not stupid questions like "How do I get there?". But maybe questions like, "I was thinking of going by chauffeur-driven limousine and putting it on expenses, is that okay?", because that affects me, as the budget holder. Maybe questions like, "Is there a dress code?", because that affects the appropriateness of the decisions you take.

Questions like this are okay because they are questions to establish the boundaries. Within those boundaries you can decide for yourself.
If we can apply this thinking to our everyday lives, why do we expect something different when we work on software?

What happens to our ability to think for ourselves when we walk through the office door?

Is it a lack of skills or knowledge? I doubt it.

Is it laziness? Maybe, sometimes, but generally I doubt it.

The answer, I think, is fear of failure.

If I let someone else do the thinking, no-one can blame me if it's not right.

"You never told me that", "that wasn't in the spec", unfortunately are just excuses for not thinking for ourselves.

Agile teams should be empowered. Empowered to make decisions for themselves. But being empowered requires team members to accept it, to use their own judgement and initiative, and to take responsibility. Go on, grasp the nettle. I dare you.

Self-Organisation Is Not Boundaryless!

One of the key principles of agile software development is that agile teams must be empowered.

In Scrum, an agile management methodology, this is known as 'self-organisation', or 'self-organising teams'.

The concept is that the team is given full responsibility for delivery and the management role on the team, known as 'Scrum Master', is a facilitator role.

The Scrum Master is responsible for orchestrating and enforcing the process (i.e. Scrum), and removing any impediments that hinder the team's progress.

For some, this is management. For others, management means telling people what to do and how to do it.

In reality, I think all teams benefit from this kind of light management style. It's empowering for team members. And, in my experience, empowered teams are more motivated and deliver better results. However - empowered teams can also take the 'wrong' direction. And to avoid this, a manager must coach and guide, and on occasions enforce a particular direction.

Self-organising teams are likely to have a much narrower view than their managers, who have broad exposure to all sorts of operational and organisational issues. They may also take a route that is contrary to important company policies. They may unknowingly take a route that has legal implications. They may take a route that suits the team and their current project, but is completely contradictory to some wider or longer term organisational goals.

So, whilst I believe strongly in servant leadership - believing that managers need to turn their thinking upside-down and work for their teams - self-organisation is not boundaryless!

What If An Agile Team Member Won't Play Ball?

What do you do if someone in your agile development team is simply not playing ball? Particularly if their behaviour is counter-productive to the key principles of agile development and is affecting the team's performance.

One comment I've heard (not at my organisation by the way) was to apply the self-organised nature of Scrum and allow the team to raise the issues with the person directly and use peer pressure to make them feel uncomfortable in the hope they might leave. Admittedly in this case the person's behaviour sounded particularly bad, but in any event this is not a good approach.

I've managed software development teams for many years (in the UK) and including large groups of over 100 people. I think I've experienced every HR/management procedure in the book and keep promising to write a book about some of the more extreme examples (that are entertaining stories in hindsight but certainly weren't at the time!).

To be honest, I found the idea of the team raising the issues as a group in the hope you wouldn't need to fire him (presumably meaning he might jump) quite alarming.

Firstly, in UK employment law he'd potentially have a case for constructive dismissal if he knows his rights or gets good advice, and that carries quite a stiff penalty. Secondly there's the issue of it not being appropriate to bully colleagues into leaving, even if they're a complete pain in the backside!

I recently wrote a short blog post about an amazing statistic I heard; one consultancy firm suggesting you could lose 25% of your developers when moving to Agile Development.

The reality is that not everyone in your team will agree with the philosophies of agile development and some find it practically very difficult to adapt to the very dynamic nature of the process and the lack of clarity and certainty it can bring.

In my experience there's only one way to deal with someone behaving badly in an agile development team (in fact in any team):

- Any discussions must be 1:1 - air dirty laundry in private not in public.

- Explain that the person appears to be finding the agile development approach difficult or appears not to be on board.

- Outline why you think that's the case, using constructive examples of how his behaviour is affecting his performance and the performance of the team.

- Tell him what good looks like; in the above examples, how could he have responded and what might the effect have been then.

- Try to understand why they're behaving as they are; do they disagree with the principles, are they uncomfortable with the process, do they find group working difficult for some reason, or is something else bothering them? Remember bad behaviour is usually a symptom of something else.

- Adopt a supportive and understanding stance; don't use personal or aggressive language; use non-emotive words such as "I feel", "it's perceived".

- See if there is anything you or anyone else can do to help or support them better?

- If it's a case of feeling uncomfortable with the principles and process, would training help?

- If not, perhaps regular 1:1 coaching sessions where you can discuss the day's events and reflect on the situation away from the main group.

- Remember they can't control their capability but they can control their conduct. In the latter respect, insist that they do.

- It doesn't matter how small, and however bad everything else is, catch them doing something right and praise them in public (be careful not to patronise, it must be sincere!).

- If none of this works, consider whether there's an alternative role that might suit them better - remember agile is not for everyone and some excellent people don't get on with it. Remember the bad behaviours are a symptom not the cause.

- When you've exhausted all other possibilities and if the conduct issues persist, if you really are 100% committed to the agile approach, you may in the end have to resort to disciplinary action potentially leading to dismissal.

- If you have to take this path, make sure you consult your HR department and follow the appropriate process for your company and location.

Finally, and just to reiterate, personally I love the agile development philosophy, but it's not for everyone and not everyone can adapt easily to the change. Your first goal must be to change people's behaviour through education and training, followed by some open 1:1 discussions with those reacting badly to the change or finding it difficult. First and foremost, try positive support and encouragement, even when it feels like it's going against the grain.

IT People Mind Your Language!

Whether you're using agile development methods or any other methodology, language is important.

I don't mean whether you're speaking English or another foreign language. I mean the words people choose to use in the office. There are two examples of this that I find particularly irritating...

The first is how people in IT refer to themselves as 'resources'. I know that strictly speaking people are resources, but it sounds like they are commodities, and in my experience they certainly are not. If we really value people, and it's not just lip service, we would not think of people, our most valuable assets, simply as resources.

I think traditional project management methods are guilty of making this phrase normal in IT. But I don't think it helps that most companies have a department called HR.

And it's just as bad the way IT people refer to others in the same company as 'the business'. It's a strange phenomena, as though IT people see themselves as external to the company they're working for, which might actually help to explain why so many IT departments are treated like external suppliers - something that I personally think is a very unhealthy way for internal relationships to be.

Referring to IT people as 'resources' and our colleagues as 'the business' fosters an us and them culture - something that can result in resentment, and all sorts of bad behaviours that can make a place an unpleasant and uncooperative place to work. And I think IT people are the worst culprits. These phrases have come from IT, and personally I think have subtle but very negative consequences.

So the question is, are these phrases now so deeply embedded in the IT vocabulary that they can't be changed? Or can we change it?

The Power of a Whiteboard

Agile software development teams often use low-tech, manual methods for tracking their work. Post-it notes or cards on a whiteboard. Charts drawn by hand. Sketches for architecture and design.

But why, for such a high-tech industry like software development, would agile teams do this, when there are plenty of project management tools available; even tools that are purpose-built for agile software development?

Personally I can see why. I think a whiteboard offers loads of advantages over electronic tools. They are mainly soft factors, I admit, but I think a whiteboard is hard to beat.

First of all, a whiteboard is visual. And it's BIG. You can see at a glance how things are going. When you're part way through a Sprint, and most of the cards are still on the left of the board, you know it's not going so well. Or you're coming towards the end of a sprint, and the cards are mostly - reassuringly - on the right of the board, you know it's going fine.

The Burndown Chart shows you instantly whether the team is on track. And, if not, by how much. All at a glance as you walk past the board. Whether you made a special effort to look or not. The visibility is unbeatable.

When you see something in print, somehow it seems more real. I guess because it's physical. A large number of post-it notes on a whiteboard looks like a lot of work. Probably because it _is_ a lot of work! Its sheer physical presence reflects the amount of work the team is actually doing. It feels busy. It feels like a place where a lot is happening, which feels good. A long list of tasks on a project plan, or a long list of rows in a spreadsheet, simple doesn't have the same impact.

A whiteboard is also flexible. Infinitely flexible. You can put literally anything you like on it. Wherever you like. In any position, any size, any shape. Unlike an electronic system, there are never any constraints. No-one ever says you can't do something because the whiteboard won't let you.

It's fast and efficient to change. You could completely reorganise a set of cards in just a few moments. Or sketch something important in seconds.

It's also more tactile. For people that like tactile, it feels good to move a card to done. You feel a sense of ownership when you pick up a card. A business owner feels a greater sense of responsibility - real acknowledgement - when they add something to the board and take something else off the board to take it out of scope. It feels like something was actually, physically removed from scope.

It's also novel. When a team starts doing agile - and they create great visibility using the whiteboard - it's remarkable how many people want to come and look. Senior people have a sudden interest in what the team is doing. And even in the process itself. That would never happen with spreadsheets and tools! I can't ever remember a Director asking to come and walk through my project plan, or walk through my product backlog. In fact the very thought of it fills most people with dread! It just doesn't happen. But the whiteboard is interesting. It's interesting to look at. And interesting to talk about. When someone walks you through it, it's actually enjoyable.

Because a whiteboard has no set structure, it suits the way many people think. Many people think visually. Not in lists, but in shapes, sizes, colours, etc. The whiteboard's lack of structure allows the information to be organised and presented however suits.

Important information can be highlighted easily by putting it on the whiteboard. Important information is not buried with loads of other documents and files in a project folder somewhere, which few people would browse and certainly wouldn't notice in passing. Its visible nature can prompt people to remember things when they see them, rather than relying on their memory to go and look somewhere else that's out of sight.

But above all else, the whiteboard is a place for collaboration. It's a focal point. Like a campfire in days gone by. Or a fireplace in your lounge. Most team discussions happen round the whiteboard. Discussions about progress. Discussions about issues. Discussions about design. All sorts, sometimes even when the whiteboard isn't even needed. It becomes the hub of information for the team. The hub for communication and collaboration.

And last but not least, the unstructured nature of the whiteboard allows it to be be personalised by the team. The team can express itself through the things it puts on its whiteboard. It starts to show the character of the team, and therefore helps to create a visible sense of team spirit.

Tools can certainly help to organise information more efficiently. But I would challenge any tool to do all of that! I'm not against tools. Not at all. But I think they should supplement the whiteboard, not replace it. Tools should be used for things they can do that a whiteboard can't. For instance, keeping track of longer lasting information, doing calculations, searching, etc.

But personally I don't think I'd ever use tools instead of a whiteboard. There's simply too much to lose.

Agile Leadership

Selling Agile: Gaining Commitment

Building people's commitment to anything new, or to any significant change, is something that takes time and happens in distinct stages.

Selling agile is no different.

As a change leader, you need to recognise this and understand the stages people go through. You need to take proactive action to identify who is at what stage of commitment, and address it accordingly. This a critical success factor in change management.

The common stages of change that all people go through are as follows…

First, there is no awareness of the problem or opportunity. There must be contact to generate the initial awareness.

Then there is a period of confusion, which must be addressed by helping people to understand the change.

My presentation about key agile principles could potentially help with the communication for the above two stages.

Then, there will possibly be a negative perception, which may be based on valid concerns, false perceptions, or possibly based on fear of the implications. Now you must sell the need for change and the positive implications, in order to generate a positive perception. Otherwise they will make a conscious or unconscious decision not to implement the change.

They will then go through a period of 'testing', where they are establishing and assessing the validity of the change and its impact. Here they must be supported in order to avoid losing their buy-in at this stage.

Only then will they move into the stage of adoption. At this point the people who need to implement the change need to be educated. This is a good time to consider formal training.

And only then, after extensive implementation, can the change ever be really institutionalised.

So, when selling agile (or any other change), as well as identifying the need for the change and the implications of implementing it, you must also pay careful attention to the process of selling the change to all key stakeholders and team members.

Identify whose commitment is needed - not only to get approval to adopt the change, but also who is needed to implement it, and make it work in practice. Set out a clear communication plan, to ensure you gain and retain their commitment throughout these stages, until the change is successfully adopted and institutionalised.

Attention to detail and keeping sustained focus on this communication plan over a long period can be the difference between success and failure.

Why Should Your Business Care About Agile?

We all talk about agile, but what does that really mean for your business, and what does your business want from IT?

- **Value for Money** - what I get is good for what I pay.

- **Productivity/Speed To Market** - we are going as quickly as I could reasonably expect.

- **Predictability** - I know what it will cost to get what I want, and I know when I will get it.

- **Quality** - I get what I expected and it's good.

- **Transparency/Visibility** - I know what's going on and where we really are.

But what they don't really want, is lots of talk about agile, or software development methodologies!

Instead, talk about value for money, speed to market, predictability, quality, and visibility. Then they tend to get the message.

Software Delivery As A Competitive Advantage

There has never been a more important time to be outstanding at software delivery. An organisation's capability in software development is now a major differentiator. Possibly the difference between success and failure. So what's changed?

Project failure
According to various studies, almost 70% of all software projects fail. Materially fail to meet their objectives, in terms of cost, time, features, or all of the above. Traditional methods of managing software delivery have consistently failed to deliver the predictability they continue to promise.

Economic uncertainty
We are living in times of unprecedented uncertainty. Investing in huge multi-year programmes is no longer acceptable. Even if you have enough money at the start, there is no guarantee you will have enough money to finish.

Rapid pace of change
Technology is changing faster than ever before. Things are changing at a speed almost impossible to keep pace with. New, disruptive technologies don't only change the rules. They keep changing the whole game entirely.

Consumerisation of IT
People's expectations of IT have changed and have changed for good. They are higher than ever. Innovation and excellence from web technology companies in the last decade have raised the bar. Amazon, eBay, Google, YouTube, Facebook, Apple, and many more, have shown consumers how good things can be. Consumers now expect technical greatness from every company they deal with. They have high expectations that are difficult to meet. And they are disappointed when they don't get what they now expect.

The need for speed

All of this is driving an incredible need for speed. A need to be faster to market with new ideas. Faster to keep up with expectations. Faster to compete. And that's why software delivery is a key strategic issue for virtually every company on the planet. Software is powering almost every aspect of the world we live in today. Faster delivery of a great user experience is not only a competitive advantage, it's a business imperative.

Software Complexity + Human Frailty + Change = ???

If we accept the above formula, why in non agile development methods is there so much emphasis on analysis, planning and control?

High level planning, such as a feature list (or Product Backlog in Scrum), and an outline plan based on the affordable team size; Yes. Otherwise you've no idea what you're in for.

But a detailed specification and detailed plan? I don't think so.

Two problems...

First, they give an artificial impression of accuracy, which given the above formula is unlikely to be possible, however firm it seems at the start.

Second, detailed analysis and detailed planning takes a long time, and given the likely inaccuracy, in my experience it's simply not worth the effort.

To successfully implement agile on an enterprise-wide scale, it's important that directors and managers believe in this reality.

Creating A Learning Organisation

Agile is often the subject of an entire transformation within an organisation. But what is transformation?

Transformation means different things for different organisations and what it is depends entirely on each organisation's own unique situation, and what they are trying to achieve. It's also something that keeps changing, as the organisation, customers and the market continues to change, and faster than ever before.

So the key transformation to create a truly sustainable successful organisation is to create a culture of continuous learning and improvement.

I have often said, if you implement nothing else from agile methods, implement retrospectives!

Look at the work of Gary Hamel, the world's leading business strategy guru, about learning organisations and the future of management, and the work of Jim Highsmith on Adaptive Leadership. In these unprecedented times of rapid change and economic uncertainty, one of the key factors in whether or not an organisation will be able to sustain success - or maybe even survive - is in its ability to respond quickly to change.

As Charles Darwin once said, "it's not the strongest of the species that survive, nor the most intelligent, but those most able to adapt". That statement is as true to business now as it was to nature then.

So how do you create an environment for continuous learning, continuous improvement and continuous innovation? How do you make your organisation a learning organisation; an organisation that is able to adapt?

One way is to show teams the power of the retrospective and the impact of creating a truly reflective and collaborative approach, and how to work as a team in order to continuously improve and innovate, and to teach teams how to do that on an ongoing basis for themselves.

That might be easier said than done, but it's one of the core benefits of agile and may be the only transformation you need!

7 Reasons Why Continuous Delivery Needs To Be A Business Initiative

One of the key practices of agile and lean teams is the idea of Continuous Delivery. If not continuous, then at least very frequent!

ThoughtWorks has an area of their web site dedicated to Continuous Delivery, and also a really interesting webinar that talks about what Continuous Delivery really means, why it's important, and how to do it - at least in principle.

Continuous Delivery might be a technical practice, but its benefits go way beyond the technical team or even the wider project. The benefits of successfully adopting Continuous Delivery could have a real strategic impact on the competitive advantage of an organisation.

Here are 7 reasons why Continuous Delivery needs to be a business initiative:

1. Build the Right Product
Continuous Delivery enables a team to get continuous - if not frequent - feedback from business colleagues, user representatives, and ideally real end users. Frequent feedback loops mean that it's possible to incorporate feedback into the build, and affect the relevance, quality and success of the end product. If Continuous Delivery extends beyond the internal organisation and is released to market, real metrics and insight can be gained from real usage, meaning that more useful features are developed further and less useful features are not. This saves wasting time on less useful areas of the product.

2. Earlier Benefits
A clear advantage of building software incrementally and adopting a Continuous Delivery approach is that some benefits can be gained much earlier, albeit in smaller pieces. Releasing some benefits early may mean generating revenue, or cost benefits, that help to fund

further development. Or they may simply give you the edge over your competition. Past experience has shown the enormous commercial power of first-mover-advantage, meaning first to market often ends up being the long term leader in their chosen space, even if their first product to market was quite basic.

3. Ability to React Quickly and Respond to Change

The only thing in life that is certain is change. It's inevitable. And things are changing faster than ever before. Two things in particular strike me as particularly challenging in this respect. The ever faster pace of technology that is almost impossible for companies to keep up with. And the economic uncertainty in the world we are currently living in. Both of these things mean that life is even less predictable than ever before. If you spend too long on anything, by the time you deliver it there is now a high chance that something important has changed. Maybe the market has changed. Maybe the customers' needs have changed. Maybe your organisation has changed. Maybe new opportunities have emerged. Continuous Delivery makes it possible to react to these changes without having a huge amount of time and money sunk into work in progress that now needs to be abandoned due to changing priorities, or worse still continues just because it's the path you are on. This also makes it more viable to react to opportunities and explore new ideas and potential new revenue streams.

4. Innovation

By combining Continuous Delivery with frequent user feedback, it is possible to get developers closer to customers or users, really aligning their understanding of what users really need and maybe even identifying things they didn't even know they needed! For instance, customers didn't originally ask Apple for an iPhone with an App Store, or for a new form of tablet computer like the iPad. Users may be reasonably satisfied with all they know is currently possible. However developers may be able to create something entirely new. This can potentially be a way to drive real innovation for your organisation.

5. Reliability & Stability

Some people worry about the risk of Continuous Delivery. In our experience of more traditional methods with infrequent releases, change is a risky thing and often leads to problems. If we adopt Continuous Delivery, won't it be chaotic and problematic and cause all sorts of quality and reliability issues? Actually, it's ironic, but the opposite is true. Continuous Delivery can enable you to deliver better reliability and stability by releasing frequently. Making changes in very small increments substantially reduces the risk of problems being caused. And keeping the changes in very small releases makes it substantially easier to find and fix problems if they do occur, minimising the time that they have an impact. The consequence of both is that Continuous Delivery teams can maintain products with even better reliability and stability than before.

6. More Efficient / Save Time

To achieve Continuous Delivery, teams need to automate deployment tasks. Often teams do not do this and the impact in terms of effort to create releases, provisioning environments and finding and resolving problems caused by differences or by lack of understanding can have a substantial negative effect. Since deployment is a task that is ideally repeated many times on a project and on an ongoing basis, it is well worthwhile to automate the process. This can lead to a lot of efficiencies and save the team time, which can then be spent developing more valuable features for users and delivering more business value.

7. Strategic Impact

Last but not least, and I guess it's really a summary of all of the above, is the strategic impact. Better products due to frequent user feedback, higher benefits due to earlier releases, greater customer focus, speed to market, business agility, innovation, reliability and more efficient. What business wouldn't want all of that?! That's why we must elevate Continuous Delivery. We must elevate it to being a key issue for executives - including non IT executives - as a critically important BUSINESS issue. An initiative to make your business as competitive as it possibly can be.

20 Qualities Of An Agile Leader

Teams of all natures - agile software development or otherwise - need inspirational leadership to perform their best. That leadership may, or may not, come from the organisation's appointed leaders. But all teams need it, nevertheless. So what are the qualities of inspirational leaders?

1. Strong communication - storytelling and listening
2. Passion for learning and intense curiosity
3. Focus on developing people
4. Having fun and very energised
5. Strong self-belief, coupled with humanity and humility
6. Committed to making a significant difference
7. Clarity of vision and ability to share it with others
8. Dogged determination and often relentlessness
9. Strong focus on priorities
10. Not afraid to show some vulnerability
11. Regular use of reflective periods to think and learn
12. Real passion and pride in what they do
13. Confidence and trust in their teams, giving them real empowerment
14. Respect for all (team members, temps, customers, suppliers and directors alike)
15. Clear standards - ethics & integrity; openness & honesty
16. Ability to drive, inspire and embrace change and continuous improvement
17. Positive attitude at all times and an innate ability to be diplomatic in any circumstances
18. Lateral thinking and ability to find innovative ideas and solutions to problems
19. Ability to inspire and motivate others
20. Willingness to take risks

These are qualities that differentiate good leaders; people others would be willing to follow.

These are also qualities of 'servant leadership'. An admirable leadership style that is particularly emphasised in agile software development methods.

How many of your team - or appointed leaders - demonstrate these qualities; the qualities of inspirational leadership?

Agile Managers Need To Turn Their Thinking Upside-Down

Managers in agile development need to turn their thinking upside down.

One way I like to illustrate the change of mindset needed for an agile manager (or should I say leader), is to think of the organisation chart upside down.

The manager works for the team. Not the other way around. Their role is to provide the necessary support to enable the team to perform consistently at their best. They do this by making sure the team has everything they need to deliver, and by removing any obstacles that get in their way or slow the team down.

Of course there are also policy and governance aspects of a managers role within a corporation, which can't be ignored or necessarily described appropriately in this way. However I think it's still a useful way to think of a managers role in agile development.

A manager also has to balance their role supporting the team with the constraints of the organisation. And manage everyone's expectations accordingly. Often, this is not at all easy, or we'd all be fab managers!

But when a manager has made this transition - made this change of mindset a habit - when it's the way they think - naturally - then they're well on their way to making the transition from manager to leader.

Lose 25% of Developers When Moving To Agile?!

I attended a very interesting web meeting a while back about SOA (Service Oriented Architecture) and agile development with the Burton Group - a consultancy specialising in Enterprise Architecture.

They said that changing Developers' mindset for agile development was one of the hardest things to do and a challenge that is often under-estimated. I've certainly seen this challenge first hand, but was very surprised to hear their view.

In their experience, they say you can expect to lose anything up to 25% of your Developers in moving to agile development, as it's just not an approach that suits everyone.

I must admit my experience is rather different. Whilst I have found educating Developers and Team Leaders (and Business people) to adapt to a different mindset takes time, actually most seem to embrace the concepts and are excited by the approach.

By contrast, I have found most tension comes with Project Managers, as it's fundamentally different to the methodology they're used to (invariably based on PRINCE2/Waterfall), and even more so Testers who like to have a lot more clarity about what they're testing than agile development usually provides.

The bottom line, though, is that you should probably expect to lose some people along the way, as agile is not for everyone.

'The Power of One'
Creating An Agile Organisation

In the past, I have often talked about the importance of "business alignment". I think sometimes it hasn't necessarily been very clear what I meant by that, so I thought I would try to explain it a bit more clearly.

By business alignment, I mean the alignment between a development team and the business unit they do work for, and the alignment of their objectives, priorities, and the way that work is managed through the delivery process.

In small organisations, these things are often inherently in line, so it seems like an academic issue - almost a case of how can this possibly be a problem? But in larger, more complex organisations, it can very definitely be a problem, particularly where organisations have historically been structured around the waterfall process and people are organised in teams by function, e.g. business analysts, project managers, developers, testers, etc.

In larger, more complex organisations like this, it can no doubt be very difficult to achieve complete alignment. This is why it's often cited as a major concern for many CIO's. How do they align the objectives and strategies of their IT departments with those of the business as a whole?

It can be hard.

It may not always be possible, or practical, to do cost-effectively, however I believe that the ideal situation is one where certain things are perfectly aligned, in one to one relationships, rather than many to one. And this I what I would say is "the power of one".

One Product = One Product Owner = One Project = One Product Backlog = One Team = One Location = One Shared Goal.

Bliss! To assure a very high chance of success, this is arguably the perfect scenario. Complete focus. Dedicated. One team with all the skills it needs to deliver from start to finish. One shared goal. All sitting together. One list of priorities.

Don't get me wrong, I completely accept and understand that for many people, creating such perfect alignment is way beyond their control. They simply don't have the authority to make this happen - certainly not across the entire organisation. And this is why I have said in the past that agile must be driven from the top. At least if you want to achieve the full transformational benefits that agile can bring.

Personally, I am lucky enough that in recent years I have always had the authority to do that, or at least something more like it. And I have no doubt that it's been a major factor in achieving the successes that I have done. It's really empowered the teams to be the best they can be.

When I think about some of the structures and processes in larger organisations, I see layers and layers of complexity. Most of which has been added over the years to compensate for organisational problems. For example, lack of alignment meaning we need to specify what's required in writing up-front and have it signed off in advance. Formal change control processes. Formal reporting processes. Etc, etc. All sorts of necessary bureaucracy in order to control the problems caused by a lack of alignment.

If only we could turn the clock back twenty or thirty years. We might have solved the problems a different way. Let's organise ourselves differently so these extra overheads aren't necessary. Let's change the structure and the way we're organised to address the root of the problems, rather than adding overheads - often in disguise as good project management practices - that are really just there to alleviate the symptoms.

I think you can successfully adopt agile principles and practices in an organisation that isn't structured in this way. And I think you will see some significant benefits. But I also think that if you structure the organisation so that development and business teams are completely aligned, the benefits of agile can be truly transformational.

The Value of Persistent Teams

As a senior manager, one of the most valuable things you can do for any development team is to create an organisational structure that enables persistent teams.

Permanent, long lasting teams; not teams that assemble for a project and then disband to reform around a new project. Particularly if projects are relatively short, it's highly valuable to keep teams persistent and stable, not to chop and change team members frequently.

When people are new to working together, all teams go through a natural process of bonding as a team. One fairly well known way of describing the stages a team goes through is 'forming, storming, norming and performing', which in summary means:

- **Forming** - when a team is first put together, the team is in the forming stage; they are polite and hold back their views while they start getting to know each other.

- **Storming** - this is the stage when people start to realise their differences and have the confidence to assert them. As people express their views, teams can argue about their differences and it's normal for a team in this stage to have a fair bit of conflict, either directly or behind closed doors. It helps to recognise when your team is in this stage, as it helps everyone to understand what they are going through and that's it's completely normal.

- **Norming** - this is the stage when people begin to compromise and the arguments or discussions turn into more constructive conversations where people learn to agree. At this stage the team are beginning to learn how to work most effectively with each other and are starting to gel as a team.

- **Performing** - it is only when the team has come through all the earlier stages that they can really start performing to their best. The speed at which they get through the previous stages varies from team to team. With some teams, they hit it off straight away and get through the process very quickly and with only a little tension along the way. Other teams remain stuck in the storming process for far too long and it's a long while before they really start performing as a team, if they ever do.

There are 3 big reasons why persistent, stable teams can make a huge difference to the performance of a development team:

Teams learn how to work most effectively together
Understanding that all teams go through this natural process is important. It helps managers to realise that it's important to give teams enough time to get to know each other, and learn how to work well together. When they have worked together for a while, they will have learnt how to optimise their skills and working relationships, and hopefully in the end they will develop a real sense of team spirit, because they actually care about each other as long-standing team members.

Teams learn how to optimise their processes
Not only in terms of their relationships, the team will also learn gradually over time how best to optimise their processes. Agile methods help with this by encouraging regular retrospectives where the team regularly discusses (and actions) what went well, what didn't and what they can do better/differently next time around. This process of continuous improvement helps a team to optimise its performance by eliminating, or at least minimizing, recurring issues that hinder the team's progress.

Teams learn how to predict their velocity
Another benefit of keeping teams stable and together long enough to optimise their relationships and processes is that they will have a known velocity. Velocity in agile methods is a measure of the speed

the team is delivering at, usually measured in points. With new teams, velocity can fluctuate wildly for a little while until it settles down, and at the outset is completely unknown. Knowing the velocity of an established team helps to plan projects more reliably.

So if persistent teams is such a valuable concept, it is best to align teams with specific products or product portfolios. That way they can move together from one project to the next without having to re-establish themselves as a team each time, and with the full benefit of already optimised relationships, processes and velocity. The idea here is about assigning projects to established teams, rather than assigning people to projects and forming a new team each time.

So what should these stable, established teams look like?

Product focused - being indefinitely focused on a particular product or set of products allows the team to gain real knowledge of the products and also of the domain, without losing this know-how and continuity each time a project is started and a new team is formed.

Business aligned - Each team should ideally have clear alignment with one area of the business, in order that they can have a very clear view of priorities and understand the wider business goals of the area they develop products for. This will help them to establish a common understanding and therefore develop stronger business relationships.

Multi disciplined - Each team should ideally include every skill required to deliver requests from start to finish. That's from the first twinkle in the eye for a new idea, right through to releasing the product for its users.

Co-located - Although it is not always possible or economic, in an ideal world the team should all be located together, not only in the same city or same building, but sitting in the same space, where they can interact face-to-face frequently as and when required.

Shared goal - Ideally a team should be focused on the same goal. Although it's not always practical to be single purpose, a team that is single minded in its aim to achieve a certain goal has a much greater chance of doing so. A team of people focused on different goals isn't really a team.

So take a look at your organisational structure. Does it look like this? What could you do to make some of these benefits possible?

How To Share An Agile Team

Scrum, and other agile development methodologies, provide a framework for managing software development projects. But all too often, methodologies focus on a project environment, where the team is dedicated to the project.

As I mentioned earlier, I favour the idea of persistent, stable teams, that remain in place indefinitely and focus on a particular set of products, rather than on a transient project.

In reality, development teams are frequently required to develop and support multiple products. Multiple products with multiple product owners. And particularly in 'business as usual' ongoing development.

So how do you share an agile product development team?

Operating as a 'resource pool' is definitely not ideal. Everyone throws their requests over the wall. Those that shout loudest get the team's attention. Or maybe the bigger products get the team's attention, at the expense of smaller products that never get to the top of the list, and never will.

Splitting the team by product sounds great. But sometimes the team would simply be too small for this approach to be practical. Or it leaves too many individual developers, causing problems with cover and you can't exactly collaborate with one developer per product!

So what can you do? I have had a similar situation in lots of my teams. Broadly speaking we have solved this issue like this:

- There is one Product Owner per product. The Product Owner maintains a separate Product Backlog for their product.

- The development team acts as one team.

- The Sprint Budget (number of hours or points available for a Sprint/iteration) is allocated to each product based on their budgetary/financial contribution to the cost of the team, for example 50/25/25%. If you don't recharge, you could agree this at a more senior level as a general rule of thumb. Each product has a known % of the budget for each Sprint, based on its current importance.

- Each Product Owner can only include Stories from their Product Backlog up to their allocated % of the Sprint Budget.

This approach means the development team can act as one team. There is cover when someone is off, because in this case the overall Sprint Budget is reduced but everyone still gets their usual percentage of the available capacity. No Product Owner is ever left with no development because their developer is on holiday.

It also means team members don't have to juggle their time between products on a 0.x FTE basis, which is awkward at best and just plain impossible when the fractions are too small or odd numbers.

Instead the tasks allocated in the Sprint are already appropriate to the Sprint Budget for the team, meaning team members can focus on delivering whatever tasks were planned in the Sprint, and not worrying about how to split their time.

C3PO - A New Role Maybe?

I've been thinking some more about the negativity I feel about referring to people as 'resources' and the fact we still call our HR department Human Resources.

Since most Board director roles are Chief something Officer, I got involved in a discussion where I suggested an alternative title for the HR Director could be CPO for Chief People Officer, which I think is very fitting and might be a good way to start avoiding this awful reference to people as resources.

But then I thought of this!

If the HR Director is responsible for People, Process and Payroll (3 P's), perhaps they should be called C3PO?

I don't know about you, but if I was CEO I couldn't resist that, and what HR Director in their right mind wouldn't want that :)

Think Big, Start Small!

Many software development projects fail simply because they are too big.

Too big to get traction. Too big to achieve clarity. Too big to stay focused. Too big to organise and manage effectively. And too big because by the time they're developed things have moved on!

A key part of agile development is the principle of building software in small, incremental releases - repeatedly iterating to continuously improve the software feature by feature. This mitigates traditional risks significantly by keeping things small, and substantially improving visibility of what's been completed.

But that doesn't mean agile development is only a good approach for short tactical work, or for business-as-usual changes to existing products. It can also be applied equally well to larger projects and more strategic initiatives, repeating many iterations before completing an entire project or release.

In this situation I would still encourage regular releases though. Certainly as regular as possible based on the minimum requirements that make sense. Why should any project only deliver 1 or 2 releases - why not deliver releases regularly throughout the project? Apart from minimising traditional risks with software development projects, this also enables early delivery of some benefits, allowing the business to realise some value early.

My mantra for keeping this in mind is "Think Big, Start Small!".

How Agile Are You?

Some time ago now, I saw a brief set of questions from Nokia to assess whether or not a team is 'agile'.

And by 'agile', I think they meant to what extent the team was following agile principles and practices in Scrum and XP (Extreme Programming), not whether or not they could touch their toes :)

I'm not sure if it was deliberately brief to emphasise the things that are the real essence of agile, but I developed the questions into a more comprehensive set of statements. A set of statements that make a fuller assessment of someone's status with agile principles and methods.

Here they are:

1. The team is empowered to make decisions.
2. The team is self-organising and does not rely on management to set and meet its goals.
3. The team commits and takes responsibility for delivery and is prepared to help with any task that helps the team to achieve its goal.
4. The team knows who the product owner is.
5. Each sprint/iteration has a clear goal.
6. All team members, including testers, are included in requirements workshops.
7. Requirements documentation is barely sufficient and the team collaborates to clarify details as features are ready for development.
8. Test cases are written up-front with the user story.
9. There is a product backlog/feature list prioritised by business value.
10. The product backlog has estimates created by the team.
11. The team knows what their velocity is.
12. Velocity is used to gauge how many user stories should be included in each sprint/iteration.

13. Sprints/iterations are timeboxed to four weeks or less.
14. Sprint budget is calculated to determine how many product backlog items/features can be included in the sprint/iteration.
15. The sprint/iteration ends on the agreed end date.
16. All tasks on the sprint backlog are broken down to a size that is less than one day.
17. Requirements are expressed as user stories and written on a card.
18. The team estimates using points which indicate the relative size of each feature on the product backlog/feature list.
19. The team generates burndown charts to track progress daily.
20. Software is tested and working at the end of each sprint/iteration.
21. The team is not disrupted during the sprint/iteration.
22. Changes are integrated throughout the sprint/iteration.
23. Automated unit testing is implemented where appropriate.
24. There is an automated build and regression test.
25. Stretch tasks are identified for inclusion in the sprint/iteration if it goes better than expected.
26. The Product Owner is actively involved throughout each sprint.
27. All code changes are reversible and it is possible to make a release at any time.
28. Testing is integrated throughout the lifecycle and starts on delivery of the first feature.
29. Impediments that hold up progress are raised, recorded on the whiteboard and resolved in a timely fashion.
30. When someone says 'done', they mean DONE! (i.e. shippable).
31. The team uses the whiteboard to provide clear visibility of progress and issues on a daily basis.
32. The sprint/iteration goal(s) is clearly visible on the board.
33. All user stories and tasks are displayed on the whiteboard for the duration of the sprint/iteration.
34. Daily scrums happen at the same time every day - even if the Scrum master isn't present.

35. The daily scrum is restricted to answering the standard 3 Scrum questions and lasts no more than 15 minutes.
36. There is a product demonstration/sprint review meeting at the end of each sprint/iteration.
37. All team members, including testers and Product Owner, are included in the sprint/iteration review.
38. The sprint/iteration review is attended by executive stakeholders.
39. There is a sprint retrospective at the end of each sprint/iteration.
40. Key metrics are reviewed and captured during each sprint retrospective.
41. All team members, including testers, are included in the sprint retrospective meeting.
42. Actions from the sprint retrospective have a positive impact on the next sprint/iteration.

I have used this effectively in multiple large organisations now. This was my approach:

- Ask every team member of an agile team (including the product owner, tester, manager, everyone) to review the statements honestly.

- Ask them to score each statement with a 1 if and only if they believe they are consistent and could be audited. In other words, if I was to turn up at any time and ask for evidence, are you confident you could provide it?

- Also, only score 1 if you believe the statement is being done reasonably effectively, at least in your opinion.

- Otherwise score 0.

- Add up the 1's for each team member. Then average the score for the team.

To what extent a team is really effective at all these points is really another matter, of course. But if a team has really got agile principles and practices consistently nailed, and according to every team member: They score 42!

We then graphed the results and discussed as a team what areas we wanted to improve. We ran workshops on the areas for improvement, looking at the reasons why they were not as we'd like and providing guidance and education about how these concepts should ideally work and why.

Several weeks later, we ran the survey again. There had been a dramatic improvement in the areas we chose to focus on, and in a very short time.

How agile are you?

Measuring Business Value
in Agile Software Development

One of the elusive things in software development is how to measure business value.

For some projects it's fairly obvious. Maybe there's a clear revenue benefit. Or a tangible cost saving. Or a very specific risk avoidance. But what about on BAU (Business As Usual)? How do you get some indication of the business value a team is delivering on bug fixes, enhancements and new features delivered as BAU?

One way - which is fairly rudimentary but an interesting indicator - is to use Fibonacci points in a similar way to Velocity.

The idea here is to put Fibonacci points for business value on every item (or User Story) on the Product Backlog, as well as the points for each feature's size.

The development team provides the points for size, because only they are qualified to judge how big a feature is, relative to another. Whereas the business value points should come from the Product Owner.

In the same way as the development team estimates in points, the Product Owner decides on a business value for each item, relative to each other. The key thing here is that the estimated business value is relative, i.e. a feature with a business value of 2 is twice as valuable as a feature worth 1; a 5 is worth 5 times a 1, etc.
When you have Fibonacci points for size and for business value, you can also do some interesting things to help prioritise your backlog. Firstly, if you have a long Product Backlog that is difficult to get your head around, you can simply enter business values individually and then sort the list by business value as a starter for ten.

Secondly, you could do a calculation of business value divided by size, which gives each feature a priority score. It's a bit rudimentary, but it's a simple way to sort the backlog so the high value/low effort features come to the top.

You can also plot this on a scatter graph, which you can set up to put the high value/low effort features on the top right, and the high effort/low value features on the bottom left. This is a useful concept and can help to facilitate a good discussion about priorities.

But aside of prioritisation, putting a business value in points against every item on the backlog allows you to calculate 'Business Velocity', i.e. how much business value (in points) was delivered in each Sprint. You could plot this on a 'burn-up chart', showing the cumulative business value delivered over time - hopefully with an accelerating trend line.

And you could use this graph to see whether the business value for each sprint is increasing or decreasing. Naturally a team's business value might slow down as a product matures in its commercial lifecycle. Maybe in this case it's time to think about switching the team onto other priorities? Maybe it coincides with a lower velocity? Or maybe it's time to think of some more valuable ideas? Either way, I guess it could be interesting to see.

Metrics

When I was a young manager, I remember repeatedly hearing people say "you are what you measure". Originally I didn't really agree with it, because I found software development such a hard thing to measure.

In contrast, I have heard other people quote Einstein who said that "Not everything that can be counted counts, and not everything that counts can be counted". Personally, that resonates more with me, and he was a clever chap!

I also worry about the complexity of metrics. Measure the 'wrong' thing and you can get some very dysfunctional behaviours that aren't at all what you intended. Or you can get people worrying so much about the metrics that they manipulate them. Not good.

As I moved up the ladder into more senior management roles, I came to the preference of measuring business outcomes affected by our software rather than measuring the software development process itself.

For example, in my last job where I was the Web Technology Director for the UK's largest consumer media company, I set out with 4 major aims. They were:

- Fast & Reliable Websites - performance and availability
- Reputation for Delivery - velocity and predictability
- Strong Business Relationships - stakeholder satisfaction
- Driving Online Growth - revenue and traffic

Each of these is in itself reasonably measurable, even though the speed and quality of our development is much more difficult to measure.

This is how we measured them…

Fast & Reliable Websites

This is a lead indicator for a media business's revenue, because apart from wanting users to have a good experience, there is a clear and direct correlation between the speed and reliability of the site and the number of pages each user consumes.

As such, it is a major driver, or inhibitor, of traffic growth, but something that is not always given the attention it deserves. In my experience, people often think growth is driven by adding more and more features. In my opinion, it is often the opposite; by delivering a really simple, reliable user experience that works really fast. Measuring this helped us to bring the appropriate attention to these areas and gave us a clear benchmark about how we were doing.

Clarity is important for most things in life. Metrics are no different. Originally we had monitoring software that gave us all sorts of stats about our 60 different brand sites. But we only got real clarity about this when we boiled it down to just two numbers. On average each month across all of our brands, how many seconds does it take for a page to load, and overall what is our percentage availability according to the monitoring software.

To our horror, the page load was 6-7 seconds, which we knew was terrible because this was a server to server time and we knew the real user experience was often far worse. Similarly we were having all sorts of capacity problems (partly due to the poor performance) and our sites' availability was often less than 98%.

Knowing these numbers brought a relentless focus on performance and drove some major breakthroughs in how to crack this problem at scale. Within 6 months, we had reduced page load times to sub 1 second and had increased availability to 99.99%. This was a massive achievement, quantifiable and a justifiable cause for celebration.

One of the ways we drove actions from the metrics was to break down the two numbers by site and to present them in a league table. With so many sites and so many conflicting priorities, we knew we

352

had to focus on this piecemeal, so we created a policy that the bottom 3 sites had to take action and put some material performance improvement work into their next iteration. As each site took action, we discovered the things that made the most difference and were able to apply these to the other sites, raising the standards for them all.

Reputation for Delivery

I really wanted my group to have a great reputation. In particular a great reputation for delivery. I joked with people that knowing whether or not we were really delivering everything that was planned wasn't important to me. I recognised the importance of expectation management and the fact that software development often isn't plannable. I didn't want the metrics to cause people to deliver things even if they were no longer appropriate. So I chose to concentrate on our reputation.

To do this, we used two metrics. Velocity and what we called Reliability, or Predictability.

We had to manage people's understanding of Velocity. It doesn't mean we're delivering the right thing, it can't improve indefinitely, and it can't be compared between teams whose own unique circumstances are different.

With this in mind, we had a graph for each team that showed their Velocity over time. This helped the team to plan based on their past Velocity, but importantly it showed our stakeholders how we were doing in terms of output, and it quantifiably show people we were getting a lot done. Which wasn't always the perception when the work was scattered across so many different business units.

It also showed initially how fast the team was improving. For several iterations, the Velocity got better and better, as the team removed its recurring impediments and became more accomplished with agile methods. Ultimately it plateaued of course, but this was not a problem as it was expected. The constant improvement in

Velocity in the meantime created a very positive feeling about the teams' progress and helped to show that we were getting better. This was much needed at the time and providing evidence of it was extremely powerful.

The second metric for Reputation for Delivery was Reliability. This was simply the number of points delivered in each iteration, as a percentage of the number of points committed in Sprint Planning. 100% was perfect, but again, we set expectations that we're unlikely to ever achieve 100% without manipulating something or padding. We focused on achieving between 90 and 110%. That was our sweet spot.

Too high a percentage means we weren't really being ambitious enough. It's easy to commit to very little and over-achieve. That might manage expectations well, but we had a lot of ambition to wanted to push ourselves much harder than that.

Too low a percentage means that some people are not getting everything they expected, so we really don't want it to drop much below 100%.

It took several Sprints for our teams to become reliable. The Reliability figure bounced up and down all over the place at first. But with the past Velocity, the figure started to stabilise after several Sprints, as the teams learned what they could really achieve and as their Velocity plateaued they become extremely reliable at predicting what they could do.

The result was that the team was respected for the fact that it had improved so much, consistently delivered good output, and consistently delivered +-10% what they said they would. Our reputation was improved dramatically and the trust and cooperation between business units and our teams grew significantly as a consequence.

Strong Business Relationships

This was a significant problem area for us at the time. Business units were in the habit of beating up the people in IT. IT people felt demoralised and downtrodden and had lost their pride and passion as a result.

It was partly caused by the above two issues - Fast & Reliable Websites and Reputation for Delivery. You can imagine the enormous improvement in business relationships that would come if your sites are fast, reliable and traffic is growing strongly as a result, and you respect the team's output and generally get what you expect. Powerful stuff.

But we did also measure this in terms of stakeholder satisfaction. We ran a very simple stakeholder survey, covering only a handful of questions so it was easy to complete.

I got the Board's support for running the survey on a wide basis and at all levels, and asked them to mandate people completing it because it was very critical feedback for us at that stage of our digital development. I still didn't get 100% response but I did get a high response and a good sample of opinions to base our metric on.

I didn't do this very often - approximately every 6 months - but it allowed me to aggregate some data to gauge people's opinion of us. As I eluded to earlier, it improved dramatically as we addressed our underlying issues highlighted by the other metrics.

Driving Online Growth

Ultimately, this was our purpose for being. So the ultimate metric was our digital revenue. But notice I didn't focus on an absolute revenue target, our aim was to grow in order to deliver shareholder value. So the metric we focused on was the growth.

In a media business, we also knew that more traffic to the websites ultimately leads to more revenue. We know the correlation isn't a straight line, as price reduces as volumes increase, however we know they are closely linked in two ways. The obvious way is that advertisers' campaigns are charged per thousand page views, so we know we need lots of page views in order to deliver campaigns. But we also knew that UK unique users was the segment of our audience that our advertisers were interested in, and growing this would allow us to compete better and win more business. So these are the two key metrics we focused on.

By focusing on UK unique users, we couldn't just use techniques for increasing page views from existing users by delivering a better user experience, we also had to get better at acquiring new users. So as you would expect in any media business, it gave us a very strong focus on SEO (Search Engine Optimisation) and Social Media (to drive referrals) and a clear way of measuring our results.

Summary

So in summary, we had a handful of extremely valuable metrics that were focused on measuring business outcomes rather than our processes:

- Fast & Reliable Websites - performance and availability
- Reputation for Delivery - velocity and predictability
- Strong Business Relationships - stakeholder satisfaction
- Driving Online Growth - revenue and traffic

Doing this helped us to focus people's attention on the results that we wanted and people's behaviour was driven towards improving these outcomes, whilst leaving the teams largely empowered to work out how.

Measuring Agile Adoption

There was one other thing we did on metrics that is worth highlighting. Based on my past experience, I had decided that agile methods were the way forward. I believed strongly that agile would help us not only to deliver better quality faster, but importantly it would help us with the specific problems highlighted in our goals: particularly the reputation for delivery and strong business relationships that were an acute problem at the time.

How we went about this is a different story altogether, but we measured our adoption with the simple survey that I explained earlier. We graphed the aggregated answer for each of the 42 questions and we relentlessly focused on improving the results in all of the areas that had a low score and felt important to us. Generally we did this through workshops, effectively training our people in various aspects of agile, over and over until the stats got better.

We measured at the beginning of our agile journey, and we measured again periodically (after about 6 weeks) as our agile adoption continued. As well as measuring the results we were achieving, I did this because it was a major change and therefore a lead indicator for the other outcome-oriented metrics. I believed they were connected. If we could get agile techniques in place and working effectively across all teams, I firmly believed the results would follow. They did, and I could measure both.

5 Reasons Why Agile Development Must Be Driven from the Top

Agile development is often initiated by the development team itself. Whilst they may find some good advantages, the most profound benefits of agile will not be realised unless it is driven from the top.

Here are 5 reasons why:

1. Multi-disciplined teams

One of the key concepts of agile development is the idea of multi-disciplined teams - "one team". An agile development team needs all the skills necessary to complete its task from cradle to grave. From initial request to delivery to market, the team should be able to deliver without reference to another team.

Having multi-disciplined teams reduces coordination, creates clear ownership and responsibility, speeds up delivery, and empowers the team. As I said earlier, profound benefits, but benefits only possible to realise often by making changes to the organisational structure, which usually needs to be driven from the top.

2. Co-location

Another key concept of agile software development is co-location. Ideally the whole team will all be located in the same place - not just the same office but literally sitting side by side in the same room or space.

Having co-located teams also reduces coordination, speeds up communication, fosters closer working relationships, creates the opportunity for continuous collaboration, enables face-to-face communication, means you can get better visibility of progress etc by putting things on the wall, and strengthens team spirit. These factors, over the course of a project, can make or break it.

Co-location often requires management intervention, in order to move people around so they can all be together. Sometimes it may be even more fundamental than that - moving people from offices in different cities and physically reorganising the company. So again, it really needs to be driven from the top.

3. Product ownership

A common problem in large organisations is that there are many stakeholders for any given product. It is also common for development teams to be developing and maintaining multiple products. The effect of this is that many people make requests, and to each of the stakeholders, their request is naturally the most important.

With so many requests coming from so many directions, how does a development team prioritise and manage expectations. Usually, it's a case of who shouts loudest! This is not the best approach for the business, as it's sometimes those demanding the most attention that get priority and not those that drive the most business benefit. It also creates an unpleasant working environment, where the default system for getting things done is to moan, shout and escalate. It's not the most motivating way to work, and it's not the most effective.

A development team needs a clear Product Owner, at least for each product if not for the whole team. The Product Owner needs to be the one person who prioritises on behalf of the business, and needs to have real authority to make decisions and stand by them. The team need to know that this is the one person they should listen to the most.

Having clear and empowered Product Owners transforms a team's performance by enabling them to work on the most important requests, cutting out a lot of noise, creating a more positive working environment, motivating the team, and strengthening business relationships.

The trouble is, in large businesses, there is often not one person who naturally holds this position and has this level of authority. The role of Product Owner needs to be explicitly assigned to someone and communicated clearly to all stakeholders. As this role often spans business units, this change usually needs to come from the top.

4. Agile project management/Stakeholder expectations

With agile project management, stakeholder expectations need to change. Where they may be used to seeing a full requirements document and/or specification up-front, they shouldn't expect to see that in agile. Where they may be used to seeing a detailed project plan in the form of a Gantt chart, they shouldn't expect to see that in agile. Unless they know that, understand why that is, and really believe in the benefits of agile and why there is a need for change, this will potentially cause you problems.

Since these stakeholders are often senior managers and directors of the organisation, these steps are an important part of selling agile and where the real change management challenge is. This needs to be carefully managed and the message needs to reach all key stakeholders, at all levels of the organisation. In order to secure real organisation-wide buy-in, this usually needs to be driven from the top.

5. Different values

Agile has different values to traditional project management methodologies. Unless people understand what these values are, and how they are different, they will struggle to adopt or embrace some key aspects of agile software development.

People need to understand that whilst they will have less predictability and won't be able to see a clearly defined fixed scope, instead they will get a high-performing team that can deliver software faster and to a higher quality, and that they'll get much more visibility and flexibility that's more likely to meet their changing expectations, and with less bureaucracy.

Everyone needs to know that it's okay to lack that perceived clarity from the outset in favour of flexibility and the other benefits that come from adopting agile development. They need to know that agile principles and practices mitigate risk in a different way - not with detailed planning and analysis and strict control, but through visibility, transparency and frequent delivery of working software in small incremental iterations.

People need to know that these values are supported from the top; that it's not only okay to behave in line with these new principles, it's expected.

Summary
Adopting agile development will help with many issues. But without these things being led from the top, you will only be partially successful and you will only see a small fraction of the possible benefits.

10 Things Agile Executives Need To Do Differently

Agile adoption is sometimes driven from the top by courageous executives boldly declaring "We're going agile!". They see a vision of a better, happier place, where development is better, faster, cheaper, and they want it. That's understandable, of course. But some don't realise the implications. When moving to agile methods, it's not just teams that need to change. Executives need to change too.

Here are 10 things agile executives need to do differently:

1. **Do Less** - limit work in progress at portfolio level, eliminate waste, create focus, do less in parallel, keep things simple.
2. **Explore & Adapt** - rather than follow a plan.
3. **Learn Fast** - short feedback loops, tolerate mistakes, value learning and continuous improvement.
4. **One Team, One Goal** - avoid silos by setting up product oriented, co-located, multi-disciplined teams with shared purpose; squash politics.
5. **Focus On Value** - focus on value over cost, deliver value earlier/incrementally, concentrate on building the right product.
6. **Empower Teams** - inspire and engage, provide opportunity for intrinsic motivators: autonomy, mastery and purpose.
7. **Accept Hard Truths** - be open, accept difficult messages, support the team in resolving them; agile doesn't solve your problems, it highlights them.
8. **Think Big, Start Small** - have the big vision, but deliver it in small bite-sized pieces.
9. **Collaborate** - play nicely, be supportive, give your people's time, actively participate in projects.
10. **Lead By Example** - be agile yourself, use agile techniques, exhibit agile principles, adopt a servant leadership style.

If you want your teams to be truly agile, take a hard look at yourself and your executive colleagues. Are you agile too? Are you setting agile up for success? Are your behaviours creating an environment where agile can flourish? This is very important if you want your teams to succeed. If you ask for agile, but your own behaviour is inconsistent with agile principles, your teams won't be able to change fully, even if they want to, and you'll only get a fraction of the benefits you could otherwise achieve.

Are you – or your executives – agile too?

IT Departments Need To Change
With The Times

The world is moving at an ever faster pace. At the same time, we have been operating in the harshest economic climate in our lifetime. The younger generation coming into the workplace take technology for granted, and use it in ways that not long ago we would never have imagined. Now we can access what we want, when we want, and how we want; wherever we might be and on whatever device. Technologies are converging (eg. web and mobile), whilst at the same time, new technologies are rapidly emerging - for instance, web TV, 3D, tablet computers, even augmented reality!

How is any organisation meant to cope with all of this?

It is no longer about which organisations have the heritage and strength to withstand all this change, but about which organisations are fast enough to respond to it, and adaptable enough to evolve with it. It is no longer possible to plan for three to five years. Nothing is constant for very long - at least not where technology's concerned.

So why do so many organisations still stick so rigidly to old conventions?

Traditional methods go back years. They worked well when things were very different. But maybe they aren't always so appropriate in the world we live in today. In an environment that is full of complexity and uncertainty, we need to structure projects differently to face that challenge.

That is why agile development methods have emerged in recent years, and why these innovative management techniques are now crossing into the mainstream. Not just in small technology companies, but in large media companies, and more recently in large corporates and government organisations too.

Whereas traditional project management methods emphasise planning and control, agile methods instead emphasise people, collaboration, flexibility, and as the name suggests, agility. For anything that is intrinsically unpredictable, because of complexity, uncertainty, or the rate of change, it is finally being recognised by many organisations that empirical, adaptive methods are more appropriate than traditional methods based on planning and control.

Agile methods also place a strong emphasis on continuous improvement. The true measure of an organisation's chances of long term success may be its ability to learn, and respond to change, and to adapt to the unforeseeable, changing circumstances ahead of it.

As innovative and empowering as agile methods can be, they do require a commitment to a fundamentally different way of thinking. To see maximum benefits from agile methods, organisations may need a different structure. That's what makes the adoption of Agile methods difficult. It's a cultural change. And it's potentially structural. It's not something that can easily be adopted in small, isolated silos, at least not if it's to achieve its full potential.

Organisational change of this magnitude ideally needs to be driven from the top, because it requires authority, commitment, leadership, and tenacity. It also requires awareness, understanding and buy-in, right across the business and at every level.

Organisations that have successfully made this change have cited transformational benefits. Agile development and agile project management methods tend to drive out a stronger commitment to delivery; to quality; to innovation; to collaboration; and to building stronger relationships with others in the business. Agile methods also help software development teams to deliver the right solution, thanks to frequent iterations, delivering in small, bite-sized pieces, and constantly inspecting and adapting based on collaboration and feedback. Agile teams embrace change, rather than seeking to prevent it.

Organisations that successfully manage this difficult transition have the opportunity to transform themselves into an agile business. A business that's ready to adapt to change. And consequently, a business that will stand the tests of time, whatever life throws at us next.

Find Out More

About the Author

Kelly Waters has over 25 years experience in software development, over 18 of which have been managing successful software development teams.

He has managed large software development departments and successfully transformed two of the UK's largest media companies by implementing agile methods in fast-moving, complex and dynamic organisations. He is currently an Executive Consultant helping other companies to do the same.

Kelly has also been a voluntary business advisor for Young Enterprise, an organisation that helps young people gain business skills through practical experience, and writes one of the most popular blogs about agile software development, "All About Agile".

To find out more about agile, visit **allaboutagile.com**.

To connect with Kelly, see his LinkedIn profile at linkedin.com/in/kellywaters

Alternatively you can follow him on Twitter at twitter.com/kelly_waters.

Further Recommended Reading

- **Adaptive Leadership paper**, by Jim Highsmith
- **Agile Estimating and Planning**, by Mike Cohn
- **Agile Retrospectives: Making Good Teams Great**, by Esther Derby and Diana Larsen
- **Agile Software Development With Scrum**, by Ken Schwaber
- **Agile Software Requirements**, by Dean Leffingwell
- **Clever - Leading Your Smartest, Most Creative People**, by Rob Goffee and Gareth Jones
- **Continuous Delivery**, by Jezz Humble
- **Implementing Beyond Budgeting**, by Bjarte Bogsmes
- **Kanban**, by David J. Anderson
- **Lean Software Development: An Agile Toolkit**, by Mary and Tom Poppendeick
- **Lean Startup**, by Eric Ries
- **Management 3.0: Leading Agile Developers, Developing Agile Leaders**
- **Simple Complexity: A Clear Guide To Complexity Theory**, by Neil Johnson
- **Succeeding With Agile: Software Development With Scrum**, by Mike Cohn
- **The Future of Management**, by Gary Hamel
- **User Stories Applied**, by Mike Cohn

Copyright © 2012 - Kelly Waters, allaboutagile.com

No part of this publication may be reproduced, stored in a retrieval system, published, or transmitted in any form, by any means; electronic, photocopying, recording, scanning or otherwise, without the express permission of the author, Kelly Waters.

Limit of Liability/Disclaimer of Warranty: The publisher and author make no representations with respect to the accuracy or completeness of the contents of this work and specifically disclaim all warranties, including without limitation warranties of fitness for a particular purpose. No warranty may be created or extended by sales or promotional materials. The advice and strategies contained herein may not be suitable for every situation. Neither the publisher nor the author shall be responsible for any damages arising herefrom. The fact that an organisation or website is referred to in this work does not mean that the author or the publisher endorses the information the organisation or website may provide or recommendations it may make. Further, readers should be aware that websites listed in this work may have changed or disappeared between when this work was written and when it is read.

Front cover image courtesy of Holly Waters.

36186112R00212

Made in the USA
Middletown, DE
26 October 2016